7

HOW TO FIX UP OLD CARS

HOW
TO FIX UP
OLD CARS

by *LeRoi Smith*

ILLUSTRATED

DODD, MEAD & COMPANY

NEW YORK

Introduction

More than ever before, the driver who can service and maintain his own vehicle is fortunate. The costs of owning and operating a car today are very high, much higher than we would like to suppose. A used car costing $500 really requires an expenditure of nearly $1000 over a span of three years. When a new car is purchased for $4000, with finance terms the monthly payment on a typical 36-month contract will soar above $100. With vehicle insurance, petroleum, and rubber products, the monthly "rent" goes up another $50 to $60. Thus, a new family car becomes the second most important purchase a man is likely to encounter, after his home. With minor repair bills, which are certain to crop up after the first three years, the cost goes up to another $15 to $20 a month. A new car is almost too expensive to own.

For the young person just starting a driving career, such expenses are obviously way out of line. Even the so-called inexpensive used car may prove to be a nightmare of hidden costs. The way to beat this high price on transportation is to carefully select and fix up an older car until it runs like a top. In this way, a maximum of $500 spread over a period of months or years will let the ambitious beginner assemble an appealingly different car that will offer several years of trouble-free travel. In addition such a car will usually bring a resale price higher than the entire investment.

That's what this book is all about—fixing up old cars. Not just restoring an old Model T Ford, or creating a shiny hot rod, or breathing life back into the old hand-me-down family bus. A broad look is taken at all the things involved in fixing up any old car, whatever the model. Throughout, the book emphasizes the important details the reader must understand if the result of his work is to give complete satisfaction.

Contents

Illustrations

HOW TO FIX UP OLD CARS

1 How to Buy an Older Car

Good old cars are where you find 'em, and locating an automobile just right for you is more a matter of search, patience, and preplanning than of sheer blind luck. This holds true whether you want a particular Model A to restore, a 1940 Chevy coupe to hot-rod, or just something to fix up and drive. Invariably, or so it seems, all the good cars have been taken, leaving a variety of thrashed offbreed brands about as desirable as German measles. Fortunately, this is far from the case, especially when the enthusiast is willing to be different, willing to create rather than duplicate, willing to have fun.

Restorers and hot rodders are particularly plagued by this apparent lack of suitable building material, since so much of both sports has been dominated by older Ford products. The 1932 Ford "Deuce" is high on both lists as most desirable, followed closely by touring cars and roadsters, then sport coupes and sedans. Finally, even the old-time Ford truck is considered fair game. Any Model A is deemed superior to the Model T,

1

while the 1933–34 is certainly more handsome to most than the 1936 or 1939. Because of this pointed attention, Fords are more in demand than other makes of old cars. At the same time, there probably still are more old Fords around, with one official source estimating over one million Model A's presently available. Locating a suitable old car to fix up is not nearly as difficult as it would seem.

Sometimes, it is hard to see the forest because of all the cars, cars that belong to friends and relatives. When such a vehicle is available, it may be the best old automobile around, especially if it has received care through the years. But if it is in poor overall condition, pass for something better. One of the cardinal rules in buying older cars for rebuilding is to start with a car in the best possible condition. This doesn't mean a super good engine or perfect running gear, because these can easily be fixed. It does mean all the small things that make up the total vehicle (some 15,000 of them in a typical automobile). In fixing up an old car you will want to put everything in top shape, including such details as rubber moldings, running boards, upholstery, and chrome trim. The better these things are to begin with, the easier (and cheaper) the job will be.

The very first step in fixing up a car is to sit down at the kitchen table and start thinking about exactly what kind of car you want and what you plan to do with it and to it. If you're not sure what the older cars look like, and how they were built, a trip to the library will turn up the answers in old magazines and books on the subject. Check the library racks for old *Motor Manuals*, which you'll find invaluable for the mechanical information needed to thoroughly rebuild a car.

All experienced car enthusiasts go through this idea stage before starting actual work, simply because it saves much time and effort in the long run.

Decide on how much you want to spend, both for the car and, afterward, for fixing it up. Determine how long you will keep the car, and how it will be used. For instance, after it is fixed up a 1952 Chevy sedan can be expected to give trouble-free service for three to five years with normal maintenance, but it will never be a Pontiac GTO in performance. A casually restored 1935 Chevy can be used for a few years of transportation, then sold for several times the original purchase price. These are things to be considered.

As a rough guide, the older the car, the more expensive rebuilding will be, but the greater will be the selling price. The more desirable the body style, the more you can expect to sell for, too. A 1939 Ford or Buick touring car or convertible sedan in average shape will bring upward of $1000, but can be bought for as little as $50 if it's in sad, unrebuilt shape.

The weather is a factor, also. The fellow in Texas isn't too concerned with rain or snow and can do nicely with a convertible, while someone in North Dakota may need a closed car. Of course, if some other dependable transportation is available, almost any style of old car can be fixed up. A roadster is unbeatable on a nice spring day!

Old cars can generally be classified in three basic categories: early—anything up to 1949; late—1949–56; and modern—1956 and later. Each can fill a particular need. For instance, an early machine may be the most desirable if a specialty car is wanted, perhaps a restored coupe or hot rod. At the same time, it may be far from the most practical. A high-school or college student might find a true restoration or hot rod much too demanding of time, especially if he wants to keep it spotless and running perfectly. In that case, he might be better off with a 1950 Ford or a 1956 Dodge pickup.

After you decide what car it will be, or what general type, the patient search begins, and it may last for months. But the wait will be worthwhile, if you are not willing to settle for second best. Again, the older the car, the harder it will be to find, and the more effort required.

During this searching operation, there are certain definite places to look. If you are after an old-timer, then look where the old-timer used to live—small forgotten towns, farms, dilapidated old buildings, unused garages. Spread the word that you are looking for a certain type of old car. Tell all your friends and relatives; drop your name and address with possible out-of-town contacts; leave notes on bulletin boards in auto-parts houses. Even advertise in the newspaper. You'll be amazed at how much information this turns up. Of course, the newer the car the less trouble you will have finding one, in particular anything made after 1948.

In choosing a car, serious consideration must be

given to the mechanical components involved. If it is a pre-1948 car, lots of work can be expected: changing the brake system, installing a late-model engine, new upholstery and paint, etc. The post-1948 automobile is usually in reasonably good shape, requiring only minor repairs. Picking the right car to begin with is the key. Nothing is more discouraging than to start on a car only to find halfway through the project that an easier, less expensive choice would have been better.

For instance, suppose a car from the early fifties is going to be fixed up. Most often, this will be either a Ford or Chevy, and probably a coupe or hardtop body style. The builder must plan on installing a late-model overhead-valve engine if he wants to keep up with the Sunday traffic. Since an engine swap costs money, it would be far wiser to consider a 1949 or later Oldsmobile. Here is a car with exactly the same basic body style as the Chevrolet, but already equipped with a strong V8 engine and one of the best four-speed automatic transmissions ever developed. Half of the problems have been solved without touching a wrench.

There are many other cars from the early fifties that can be rebuilt into excellent vehicles at a minimal cost, some with powerful enough engines, not necessarily V8's. The 1949–55 Hudson series is an excellent beginning, because the in-line 6- and 8-cylinder engines are inherently very strong, and the body takes abuse very well. Another advantage stems from enthusiasts scattered around the country who are willing to sell spare parts at low cost. A completely restored Hudson with

modern styling and good performance and handling
will cost about $400, not counting the initial purchase
price, which should not exceed $100.

Other very good cars to rebuild include the 1951 and
later Chryslers with the big Hemisphere-head V8,
Dodges and DeSotos with the smaller Hemi engine,
and the 1949 or later Cadillacs. Of the mid-1950 lineup,
the Studebaker coupe is hard to beat for appearance,
and runs well enough with the small-displacement V8.
Any of the post-1954 Ford products are excellent, since
parts interchangeability is common and installing later
engines is a bolt-up operation with no special adapters
required. The same holds true for 1955 and later Chevrolets. The Buick is not so ideal if you want to swap the
engine, but as something to fix up with stock parts it
is worth using.

If you are willing to accept the problems of an engine
swap, then body style becomes paramount. The usual
choice is a Ford or Chevy, but there is one little car
that looks tremendous and is a natural with a Chevy
283/327 or Ford 260/289 engine. It is the Willys Aero
sedan of the early 1950's. Even the Willys Jeepster, a
sort of modern-day touring car, makes an excellent
project. In the same camp, Jeeps are very popular when
equipped with V8 engines, and they prove to be one of
the soundest automotive investments.

As a rule, whenever an engine swap is required, there
will be an additional cost of $150 to $400, depending
upon the price of the engine, adapters, labor, and so on.
So you should carefully consider the end result. A 1951

Chevy coupe can end up costing $600 or $700 with a V8 engine, but it would be almost impossible to sell the car for such a sum. On the other hand, a same-year Chevy pickup with the same V8 would easily bring the high price from an adult buyer. To determine the possible resale market, watch the newspaper ads, find out how popular such a car would be with young and old alike, and balance the final result against a later model car in terms of performance. If the engine swap still seems reasonable, chances are it will be. Above all, avoid making a swap just for the romance of it.

In buying older cars, care must be exercised not to pay more than the car is actually worth. Because of the current popularity of fixing up old machines, many owners have the mistaken idea that anything old is worth a lot of money. A 1940 Packard sedan is old but it isn't a classic car by any means; "special interest" is a more appropriate tab. As such, it should bring very few dollars more than the plentiful same-era Ford or Chevy. Knowing the rarity of cars, which is a direct measure of demand and price, is essential to anyone wanting to restore a classic or antique. Unfortunately, this is such a nebulous field there can be no hard and fast rule. If the problem comes up, contact a restorer for advice. Although $400 may not seem like much for that old 1925 Model T, thoroughly restored T's are going for as little as $500! A three-dollar telephone call may save several hundred dollars.

To get an idea of the going price for any post-1949 car, talk with your local used-car salesmen. The price for a sharp 1952 Dodge will be about the same ($100) in New York as in California; however, a used Chevrolet with perfect body may bring several hundred dollars in California but no more than $50 in New York. It all depends on demand. A 1955–56 Chevrolet Nomad station wagon in good condition is worth $800 or more in areas where hot-rodding is strong, but almost valueless elsewhere. The used-car salesmen know local prices.

Prices of old cars can be grouped together, however, to give the beginner an idea of what's in the ball park and what's out of reason. The relationships between prices in the following table should hold true year after year.

Ford

Model T	$10–$500 depending upon body style and condition
Model A	Same as T
1932	$100–$500
1933–48	$100–$400
1949–60	$ 50–$500

Chevrolet

1948 and earlier	$ 50–$200
1949–54	$ 50–$300
1955–60	$300–$500

Oldsmobile

1948 and earlier	$ 50–$100
1949–60	$ 50–$600

Chrysler Corporation

1958 and earlier	$ 50–$200
1959–60	$150–$400

When buying an old car, know beforehand how much you expect to spend on repairs, then add 10 percent to cover hidden expenses. In bargaining with the seller, you have an advantage if you know exactly how much the car will cost to fix up. And get all the legal papers, as well as a separate bill of sale. They will be necessary for subsequent registration.

The ultimate cost of fixing up an old car will depend in large part on exactly how much work you do personally and how well you learn to shop for good used equipment. A later chapter is devoted to buying used parts, with hints invaluable for keeping the price down.

Usually, a car built before the Second World War will require a complete engine overhaul, as well as transmission and rear-end work. The engine will cost from $50 to $150, the transmission and rear end from $25 to $50. A brake job will be an extra $25, and front-end or steering parts will cost between $10 and $25. New tires will almost certainly be needed and will run $15 to $20 each. A paint job will cost anywhere from $20 to $100 depending on how much of the preparation you do yourself. Body and fender work is impossible to estimate. Upholstery runs true at approximately $275 for sedans, $200 for coupes, and $150 for roadsters. Do your own upholstery and you can subtract 60 percent.

With this cost information in mind, it's easy to see that with Grandmother's old 1939 Plymouth you can run up a tab of $500 very quickly. If you are a careful and patient mechanic, this can be cut to $200 or less, by using used parts and doing all your own work. Much money might be saved by shopping for a better old car.

That Olds Rocket in good shape for $250 might be cheaper in the long run.

Learning how to approach wisely the cost of fixing up an old car can be as valuable an experience as the actual mechanics. Sometimes, it's almost as much fun.

2 Buying Used Parts

Anyone experienced in working on cars considers the automotive wrecking yard his most valuable ally. There are some tremendous values beyond those high tin fences. Whatever you call it, wrecking yard, junkyard, auto dismantler, or what not, the final resting place of a nation's discarded transportation fleet is a veritable mechanical gold mine.

A junkyard is nothing more than an automotive secondhand store, where you can buy slightly used (or perhaps abused) merchandise. It's a place where cost and availability are the predominant factors—cost because the price asked or paid is much lower than for a similar new item, and availability because so many automotive parts for cars three or more years old are hard to find anywhere else.

The junkyard operates like any other business, with a wholesale and a retail price structure. The retail price of a used part may be one-half new part cost. A further saving is passed along to bonafide garages. If you have a friend in the business you may be able to save from 10 to 30 percent over the already low cost. The point is, a wrecking yard is a business, just like a service station or new car dealer, not just a muddy field covered by overturned wrecks.

Wrecking yards come in all shapes and sizes, from one-man postage-stamp operations to great bustling warehouses covering acres of ground. The former is likely to be a lackadaisical affair, with little attempt at organization, while the latter is almost always efficient. In either case, it behooves the old-car rebuilder to introduce himself to the owner. It is not the general policy of junkyards to allow browsers, but when the owner knows you're a solid customer interested in finding a part, the barrier is usually dropped.

There are certain auto parts best purchased new, and others that will do just as well used. This is one area where the beginner gets into trouble fast. In an attempt to save money, he sometimes buys a carburetor or fuel pump from a junkyard under the assumption that these parts came from a running car and therefore are good. Such is seldom the case. Carburetors and fuel pumps, as well as coils, should always be purchased new. Although a rebuilt carburetor is not the best bet, it may prove even less expensive than a used carb from the wrecking yard in the long run.

All electrical items purchased from a junkyard should be inspected carefully. You're not going to get a guarantee on any of these parts, although the yard operator will normally exchange a part if it proves defective within a week or so of purchase. When buying a generator, starter, regulator, etc., check the general exterior appearance, keeping in mind that outside grease does not necessarily indicate the internal condition. If the pulley on a generator or alternator is bent, the unit may or may not be operative, and in such a case you may be able to buy the item cheaply. If there is any question of impact, inspect the case thoroughly for cracks.

The interior can be checked by looking at the brushes and commutator. Brushes worn down more than one half their width indicate a starter-generator in service for roughly 30,000 miles or more. If the commutator is not bright, look further for excessive commutator wear. If there are signs of solder on the inspection band, the unit has been excessively hot and is not a good risk.

You can check most electrical components before you buy, and the yard operator would prefer that you do. The generator can be mounted on a runable engine, which takes some time, but the starter is easily checked by grounding the case and attaching a battery lead. This will reveal a dragging armature or inoperative Bendix drive. Grounding a voltage regulator and installing external battery power will let you know whether the points are working.

Except for carburetors, fuel pumps, and possibly some of these electrical components, just about everything on a car will work as well used as new—with the major exception of the brakes. Here is one vital area where you can't afford to play around. *Never* buy used wheel cylinders or used brake shoes! New ones cost very little. Brake drums should be inspected for excessive wear, since too great a gouge in the drum would necessitate turning it down too thin. At the same time, don't buy a drum that obviously has been turned very thin previously. Always have used drums turned by a brake or machine shop before you use them. Other brake parts, such as backing plates, lines, and master cylinder, may be used after a thorough cleaning and inspection. Particularly look for bad lines, and if the master cylinder has gone unused for some time, or is rusty and possibly leaking, definitely rebuild it.

A large safety factor is built into American cars, so parts can withstand considerable abuse or impact without failing. This means you can buy most chassis parts from a wreck with confidence. Just because the part is from a fifteen-year-old car doesn't mean it is worn out.

Probably the most difficult thing about finding used parts for the older car is simple supply. As sure as shooting, when you break the franastat on your Whipple, there won't be a wrecked Whipple anywhere. However, if the rear end of something rare, such as a 1954 Jaguar, fails, there are often parts from another car that will fit. Check with the wrecking yard's *Hollander Manual*. This invaluable big book is chock full of information on parts interchangeability. It tells the junkyard owner that a late-model Chevrolet rear end will fit that Jag, and that certain parts of a VW will work on a Porsche, and that Cadillac rods interchange with Chrysler, etc. All this is so because car companies like to buy or design various vehicle parts around standard sizes; as a result, they make similar rod bearings, similar universal joints, similar wheel bearings.

Even when you know what you want, or a good substitute, you may have trouble finding it in any one wrecking yard. For this reason you must learn what kind of junkyard to patronize. For instance, if you need a bumper for an old pickup truck, or steering gear for a 1935 Ford, don't expect to find this at a relatively new yard. Instead, look for a yard that has been around for fifteen or twenty years. By the same token, the older yard may not have a wide selection of later model cars.

If the yard is modern, chances are the owner is in direct contact with other yards throughout the city, county, or state. Most wrecking-yard people belong to organizations formed specifically for locating parts. Say you want a front fender for your 1955 Chevy, but the wrecking yard in your town doesn't have one. The operator will get on the telephone or teletype and within a few minutes tell you exactly who has the item, what condition it is in, and how much it will cost.

Even if you cannot locate the part you need in a junkyard, always tell the yard workers what you want. They often know where the unusual is to be found.

You may be in a junkyard because the particular part you need is no longer sold by new car dealers, but you probably will shop there because of price, the most valid reason. It is much better to pay only one quarter new-part price and then spend a few moments cleaning the part.

Before visiting a junkyard, it is wise to have a good idea what new-part cost is. This entails little more than a visit to an auto-parts store or dealer. Most wrecking yards are completely honest, but occasionally an unsuspecting buyer will be stuck for more than a part's value, intentionally or otherwise. For instance, if you need a transmission from a Falcon, you should know that they are common and sell new at an unusually low price. The junkyard owner may quote a flat fee above the proper price. In the case of the Falcon transmission, you might hear "fifty bucks," but if the yard owner were to take the time to look in his book he would see the new price is only $30. If you don't remind him, you're the loser.

The price you pay for a used part will be determined by several factors, including the wholesale price of a new part, the wholesale price of a rebuilt part, how easy the part is to remove, and the availability of the part in your area. Also involved is the amount of work required to make the part reusable. This last factor usually concerns body panels more than mechanical parts. Mechanical and electrical parts are generally cheaper than body parts, comparing new and used prices, simply because mechanical and electrical rebuilts are more plentiful.

When buying used parts, you won't want to pay more than 60 percent of the new list price. Mechanical and electrical items should go for half the rebuilt and one quarter the new price. Take the cost of a late-model starter. New it may cost $50, but the wholesale price

is $30. A rebuilt starter will run $25 retail and around
$15 wholesale. The junkyard owner will sell a used unit
to a garage for around $5. This much saving is neces-
sary for the professional mechanic, because if the
starter fails he will have to replace the defective unit.

Just because you're not a professional mechanic
doesn't mean you won't get a break, too. That same
starter will only cost you between $8 and $9, because
the junkyard owner must rely on return business. Like
the gas-station operator, he wants to create a steady
clientele, even if a customer comes in only two or three
times a year.

If you are wondering how a junkyard can sell used
parts so cheaply, it is because their investment is so
small. When a car is wrecked and totaled out by the
insurance company, the wrecking yard pays very little
for the entire hulk. The price is set on a sliding scale,
dictated by the model's year: A one- or two-year-old
car will cost upward of $600, while a three- or four-
year-old will go for $250 or less. Cars over six years
old are bought for a song. Suppose a wrecking yard
buys a totaled Cadillac for $500. The engine and trans-
mission can be sold for between $250 and $600. The
rear end will bring an additional $75 to $100, the front
suspension components perhaps $50, etc. Usually there
is some reusable sheet metal, worth upward of $400.
By the time all the usable parts are sold, the yard owner
has more than doubled his cost.

Always get a receipt! This is important for a number
of reasons, not the least of which is proof of ownership.

If a person has a legitimate part for sale, he will have a receipt for you. Never buy anything if you suspect it is stolen. An immense number of automotive parts are stolen in this country, especially high-performance or "fad" equipment, such as four-speed transmissions, mag wheels, bucket seats. You'll be very discouraged if you shell out money for a hot piece of gear, only to have the rightful owner reclaim it later.

Body Parts

This is one area where the individual, whether a casual mechanic or professional rebuilder, can save a good deal of money—not because he is buying a used part, but because this will encourage him to fix his own car. A large portion of a modern body man's charges are for "remove and replace."

Many body panels are interchangeable, which makes the finding job easy. Sometimes you will have to settle for a panel with a small hurt, but having this repaired or doing it yourself is far cheaper than a total repair job would be.

One caution about buying sheet metal: make sure you're getting panels that have not been previously repaired. They might look all right, but were straightened to fit another car, and may not fit yours. Incidentally, always buy a complete door rather than just a panel. All you need then to make it match your car is paint and new upholstery panels.

Chassis Parts

Unless a wrecked car was hit directly on the chassis part you need, chances are the part is still good. In a front end collision, much of the impact is absorbed by the sheet metal and frame extension. If the impact is severe, the frame generally buckles behind the suspension-mount points, but the A-arms, shocks, springs, wheel assemblies, etc., usually escape serious damage. The rear end is more susceptible, especially in a severe rear-end collision or hard blow directly on one of the rear wheels.

The steering assembly usually escapes serious damage, but the older the car the more worn the parts are likely to be. One good way to get an idea of steering-gear condition is to check the wheel for play, which should not exceed half an inch.

Radiators

Here is another item on which you can save a bundle of cash. Fortunately, because a radiator is really quite flexible, it can bend and change shape without being seriously damaged. In many cases of front-end damage, the radiator will be pushed back into contact with the engine fan, but even if the fins are badly mauled, the tubes may remain unscathed. The only way to check a radiator is by filling it with water. If it is a late-model unit (post 1955), the kind that operates with up to 21 pounds of internal pressure, some small pinhole leak might not show up at first. In this case, have a radiator shop pressure check the unit before purchase.

Engines

Engines found in a wrecking yard are either a boon or a bust, depending upon the buyer's ability to select. However, since engines make up a major part of a junkyard's resale business, the yard owner wants you to be satisfied. For this reason, he will not intentionally sell you a bad one.

You can hook yourself into paying more than necessary if you're not careful. For instance, only the neophyte will wander into a yard and ask for a Corvette engine. This request immediately marks him as short on mechanical know-how. He may be sold a genuine Corvette engine for what seems an appropriate price, although an ordinary Chevrolet V8 going for $100 less is the same basic thing.

Always know exactly what you want to buy, and check with a mechanic if you're not sure. *Motor Manuals* list where and what the appropriate identification numbers are, so you can tell one engine from another merely by comparing serial numbers.

The condition of an engine is usually the direct result of mileage on the car, but the engine is not always in the original chassis. If the engine is installed in a car and you can hear it run, all well and good. Otherwise, you will have to rely on general appearance, which varies with miles of use. Just because an engine is coated with dirty grease doesn't mean it's a junker, nor does a spic and span block foretell eager newness. Ignore the cleanliness of the outside for the time being and look into the carburetor throat. If it is stained reddish brown, chances are good that the engine has been cared for. A black stain below the choke butterfly is an indication of a tired engine.

Some junkyards take great pride in keeping their premises looking neat and include a large indoor display of used engines. The engines are usually steam cleaned before display, so you have to rely on internal appearance here. Don't get stuck with a supposedly new or newly rebuilt engine just because it's clean and painted. The gaskets are a dead giveaway; if you don't see fresh gaskets beneath the valve covers and between pan and block, suspect some tomfoolery.

Also check the engine accessories. Generator brushes and ignition points, ignition wire and plugs, water-pump inlet and outlet (look for excessive rust buildup), starter and oil filter—all will show wear and abuse directly proportional to the engine's present condition.

Few yard operators will object if you want to take an engine head or pan off to check condition. After all, since you're doing the work, they aren't losing a thing. Then, if you find a flaw, they are that much ahead.

The first place to look is under a valve cover. Thick and gooey or hard sludge buildup indicates that the engine has been run a long time without care, perhaps on very short trips. Look under the intake manifold and valley cover for the same sludge, and while the manifold is off, check the intake ports for heavy carbon buildup, which indicates faulty valves.

Pull one of the heads and check cylinder-wall taper, a measurement that shouldn't exceed 0.008 inch unless the engine is to be rebuilt. Look at each cylinder wall for black streaks, which indicate excessive ring blow-by. If the walls are severely scratched or gouged, a piston or ring has failed. If the lower ends of the cylinders look as if they have been too hot (metal discolored), the lubrication control has been bad. Finally, check the little ledge around the top of the bore. If this ring ledge is pronounced, the engine has seen lots of miles.

Piston damage is obvious, as is valve condition. However, if only one or two valves are bad and the rest of the engine appears good, it is a bargaining point in your favor. You can do your own valve job inexpensively.

Checking the bottom of the engine is vital, especially if you are not convinced the engine is good. If the oil-pump pickup screen is covered with sludge, beware. With a bar, move the crankshaft fore and aft and check for excessive end play. Wrap a finger and thumb around a connecting rod and rotate the crankshaft a few degrees. You will be able to feel a little play, but anything more than a whisper is too much.

Transmissions

Transmissions, whether manual or automatic, can be a bag of snakes to the unwary. Again, outside appearance is not a good indication of inside condition, so expect to do a partial disassembly. If it is a manual transmission, first turn the input and output shafts to check for bearing damage, which will be obvious. If the tailshaft seal is bad, grease will be spread over the lip of the tailshaft housing. Next, look the case over closely for cracks, even tiny hairline breaks that are harbingers of future bad luck. If you are looking at one of the four-speed transmissions, also check for cracks around the coverplate shifting-fork bosses.

You can get a very good idea of transmission abuse from the tailshaft spline condition. Although you can't see this area, just slip a driveshaft yoke onto the shaft. If the yoke will slide all the way forward on the tail-shaft, the splines are good and have not been twisted.

Move the shifting levers by hand, and if they move freely with no hard spots or catches, that is another good sign. Pull the coverplate off and check the synchros for wear. It is a big disappointment to install a transmission only to find it shifts like a tractor. Rounded corners on the brass synchros and worn teeth inside the synchro sleeve mean a rebuild is necessary. Naturally, chipped or worn gear teeth make a transmission undesirable. As a final transmission check, look for gritty grease, which indicates that something unhappy has been happening inside. Although this may not cause apparent damage, the grit gets into the bearings and bushings, with eventual failure only a matter of time.

Automatic transmissions are harder to check. The

obvious thing to look for is a cracked housing, common-
place in the newer aluminum cases. Remove the inspection coverplate and check the oil. If the oil isn't viscous,
chances are the transmission has been run very hot,
which in turn means the clutch discs are probably worn
out. This automatic transmission oil will also lose its
distinctive smell if it has broken down. Broken or loose
bands show up right away, even to the casual eye. If
doubt lingers, remove the torque converter. Most initial
damage to an automatic shows up in the converter,
front-pump area, and if the converter has been dragging on the pump, or similar problems have been caus-
ing clearance trouble, the pump support will appear
burned.

Always replace the front and rear seals of a used
automatic, unless it is from a brand-new car. There is
a certain element of risk involved in buying a used
automatic, a risk possibly offset by prices normally $50
or more below rebuilt cost (wholesale). However, on
some transmissions scarcity can keep the price high.

Rear Ends

The backyard mechanic seldom has trouble working
on a rear end, if removal and replacement is the only
problem. For this reason, there is good traffic in rear
ends, and wrecking yards usually have a wide variety
to select from. There is much interchangeability, from
complete housing to minor internal gears and bearings,
so the *Hollander Manual* is handy once more. Visual in-

spection is the best guide when selecting a used rear-end assembly.

Rear-axle bearings can, and do, fail on the finest of new cars, so always expect to replace the bearings on any rear end over three years old. This is just good inexpensive insurance. While looking at the bearings, inspect the axles for twist (which shows up in the splines) and straightness. To check the ring and pinion for wear, put white grease on the ring gear and rotate the assembly several times. The pinion will remove the grease from the ring-gear teeth at point of contact. If the wear is correct the pattern will be constant along the tooth, slightly heavier in the middle. If the wiping is heavier at either end, the rear end is either faulty or needs adjusting.

Tearing of the teeth shows up as pits on the tooth near the base, caused by an offending sharp tooth that tears into the receiving tooth. Buying special rear ends is a problem under the best of conditions, and you can usually expect to do some rebuilding before getting perfect service.

High-Performance Equipment

Because of the great variety of high-performance cars now manufactured by Detroit, it is possible to do some special shopping in junkyards and outfit your car at a fraction of new-part cost. Don't, however, expect to find a junkyard that doesn't know what these parts are worth. It is more common to find a yard operator who grossly overrates his product value. Where he may think a three-carburetor manifold for a specific engine is worth $100, it may be a poor unit not even worth $25! Thus, you've got to know high-performance equipment before shopping.

Trading

You can do a lot of trading with a wrecking yard, sometimes much to your advantage, but this must be set up on an individual basis with the owner. Also, while some yards don't want what you have to trade, others do. Learning to buy from a junkyard is a talent, but one you'll find very rewarding.

3 Fixing Up the Engine

Fixing up the engine so it will run well is perhaps the most important aspect of rebuilding an older car, whether that car is two or twenty years old. Unlike some phases of vehicle reconstruction, engine work is strictly mechanical, with the final results a direct consequence of each and every step taken. Rebuilding an engine is like using building blocks; if one block is placed incorrectly, the entire structure may topple. Attention to detail, to each small procedure, is the secret of a successful engine job. There are basic rules to follow, and an amateur can get professional results if he pays attention to them.

The engine is probably the first thing repaired or rebuilt on an older car, and to beginning mechanics, it often seems complex far beyond human understanding. However, when you know how each engine part is related, this mechanical Hydra soon loses all mystery. It is then merely a problem of getting each part in the correct location with the right clearances and bolt-nut torque values.

Torque and Horsepower

An internal-combustion engine produces power by converting energy—the chemical energy of fuel is transformed into mechanical energy that turns the rear wheels. While the wheel may have released man from bondage, the engine has been his salvation. An engine can be used for all manner of work, work far in excess of a single individual's ability. For this very reason, engine development has taken myriad routes down through the years, with designs created for specific purposes. This is definitely true in automobile power plants. A Volkswagen engine developing 40 horsepower can shove the little German "beetle" along at 70 miles per hour and still get over 30 miles per gallon. The VW is made expressly for economical transportation. On the other hand, a big overhead-valve V8-powered limousine is not designed for economy, but for maximum comfort. Its engine will be smooth, with lots of midrange torque. Finally, a 1000-horsepower racing car needs an engine that can push it along fast. Economy, smoothness, and even mechanical life-span are secondary.

For any engine, two terms are widely used to express power output—torque and horsepower. A knowledge of each is essential to anyone working with engines. Torque is the twisting or turning force exerted by an engine's crankshaft and is measured in pounds-feet. If a lever one foot long could be attached momentarily to the center of a turning crankshaft and the force measured at the end of the lever by a scale calibrated in points, the torque could be read directly in pounds-feet because the force would be exerted at one foot of leverage from the center of rotation. Torque is an essential element in calculating horsepower and represents the force or energy available. It does not, however, represent the rate at which the force is exerted. A combination of the two represents an engine's horsepower output.

Horsepower describes the rate at which the torque or twisting force developed by an engine is put to work to produce power. James Watt, the inventor of the reciprocating steam engine, established the present standard measurement of horsepower in 1873 by determining the maximum load a strong dray horse could move in one minute. Watt set this value at 33,000 pounds moved a distance of one foot in one minute. Thus, one horsepower is equal to 33,000 pounds-feet of work done in one minute or 550 pounds-feet in one second.

Engines are tested for their torque and horsepower outputs on a dynamometer. A modern engine dynamometer is essentially a device used to apply a load to the crankshaft of an engine. This load may be applied by connecting the engine shaft to the armature of an electric generator or to a turbine wheel that churns water in a closed housing. In the case of the electric unit, the applied load is controlled by introducing an electrical resistance into the generator's field circuit. The load introduced by the hydraulic type is controlled by raising or lowering the water level in the housing.

In both cases, engine power is converted into heat and dissipated outside the dynamometer.

The loading device in a dynamometer is pivoted in a cradle so that it can rotate within small limits. This rotation is constrained by a series of adjustable weights in a platform-type scale or by a spring balance. The torque is measured directly on this scale or balance. The scale on the dyno measures only the torque at various engine speeds, and the horsepower is calculated from this factor.

Horsepower developed by a nonrotating object is calculated by applying Watt's formula: horsepower equals the force in pounds multiplied by the distance moved in feet divided by 33,000. This is for one minute. For a period of one second 550 is substituted for 33,000. To calculate the power developed by a rotating object it is necessary to change the lateral movement of an object in the Watt formula to a circular movement. To understand this conversion, it is helpful to remember that the torque exerted by a rotating body such as an engine crankshaft is measured at a distance of one foot from its center.

To effect this formula change, the factor of two times pi is added. Pi is the ratio of a circle's circumference to its diameter and has a constant numerical value of 3.1416. A circle's circumference is found by multiplying its diameter by pi or its radius by 2 pi, or 6.2832. Thus, the end of a lever one foot long would pass over a distance of 6.2832 feet in describing one revolution.

If an engine were producing 200 pounds-feet of

torque, the work output would be 200 $\times$ 6.28 or 1256 pounds-feet for each revolution. If the crankshaft were turning 3600 revolutions per minute (rpm), this would be 60 revolutions per second. Thus, 1256 pounds-feet multiplied by 60 revolutions per second equals 75,360 pounds-feet of work per second. Dividing this by 550 gives a rating of 137 horsepower.

When an engine is tested on a dynamometer, the horsepower and torque output are plotted graphically against the crankshaft rpm from minimum to maximum engine speed. The curves plotted for typical stock-car engines show somewhat similar characteristics. The torque curve usually reaches a maximum at medium engine speeds and falls off at both low and high speeds. The horsepower curve starts at a very low value, but keeps climbing with the engine speed until it reaches a peak close to the upper limit of rpm range. At this point the horsepower curve also begins to fall off and usually has a lesser value at the absolute peak of engine speed.

Since the torque curve in the average stock-car engine peaks near the midpoint in the rpm range, this is probably the point where the engine functions with the greatest efficiency. The "breathing" of the fuel and air mixture is easier at this point, the combustion of the mixture is more complete, heat losses are small, and internal friction of pistons and bearings is not excessive.

At lower speeds the torque falls off because a modern automobile engine is not designed to function efficiently at 1000 rpm and thereabouts. Breathing is not efficient because the valve timing is adjusted for optimum efficiency at higher speeds, a lack of mixture turbulence in the cylinders impedes quick combustion, and there is time for combustion heat to leak away through the cylinder walls.

At very high engine speeds, the torque in a stock engine may fall off for a great number of reasons. Usually the effect of restrictions in the manifolding and ports become more pronounced so that the engine draws in less fuel-air mixture on each intake stroke, and valves may "float" and not seal properly. The efficiency of most stock ignition systems drops off rapidly with high speed, and internal engine friction shoots up roughly as the square of the speed. In other words, the friction may be four times as great at 4000 rpm as at 2000 rpm. Many modified engines lose more than 100 horsepower in friction above 5000 rpm.

An engine is a mechanical compromise; therefore it cannot work at maximum efficiency throughout the rpm range. This is evident from the variety of engine designs available for different jobs—a diesel engine is best suited to heavy-duty construction; a small gas engine is better for the family car—and the number of different engines available for a specific automobile. Within the framework of a single car-design series there may be several engine options, from an economy in-line 4-cylinder to a super-powerful V8. Each design will do a particular job, none will do everything.

When an older engine is being rebuilt, it must be remembered that driving requirements for that engine were considerably different than they are today. High-speed freeways require much stronger engines than the low-speed roads of two decades ago. The potential for very high performance is just not in the older engines, with exceptions. Therefore, the old engine should not be expected to perform as a modern engine will.

Working on the Engine

Before you attempt to rebuild any engine, you should have all the necessary specifications available, such as clearances and torque values. More than any other part of the process, how closely you follow these figures will determine the success or failure of the job.

Cleanliness is vital. It will not insure a perfect engine job, but if the shop area is clean, the mechanic will probably pay more attention to doing a good job. Of course, a shop is not always available, but even an outdoor work area can be kept uncluttered and reasonably free of grease and dirt.

It is advisable to remove the engine from the chassis for all rebuilding jobs, otherwise the tendency is to leave some small job undone. Besides, much of an overhaul is easier to do with the engine out of the car. As a rule, an engine can be removed, overhauled, and replaced faster than a minor in-car overhaul can be accomplished.

How Much Will It Cost?

The cost of rebuilding an engine will be directly proportional to the number of cylinders involved; a 4-banger Model A will cost about half as much as a modern overhead-valve V8, etc. The basic costs are for parts, with some machine work taking a slice of the budget. A simple overhaul will require at least piston rings, main and connecting rod bearings, gaskets and seals, and a basic tune-up kit for ignition and carburetor. More often, also required will be a cylinder bore job, crankshaft turning, rod alignment, new pistons, new valves, and miscellaneous external equipment such as water pump.

To get a rough idea of what an overhaul will cost in terms of parts alone, these V8 prices are normal: rings, $20; bearings, $20; gaskets, $10; pistons, $8 each; crankshaft regrind, $20; rods reconditioned and aligned, $25; cylinders overbored, $25; camshaft gear and timing chain, $15; cylinder heads resurfaced, $10 each. It is easy to see, then, that a decent overhaul job is going to cost at least $75 to $100 for parts alone. Of course, a make-do repair will get the engine running, but life expectancy and dependability can never be gauged in this circumstance.

The cost of replacement parts can be trimmed considerably through buying wholesale, which is often possible by going to a friend in the auto-repair business. Parts-cost markup is generally from 40 to 60 percent, which means a big saving. The cost of machine-shop labor for boring and such is not marked up as much, although the professional mechanic does get a discount.

The real saving in doing your own engine work is in the labor charge, which may run as high as $10 an hour at some garages. Roughly half the cost of an engine rebuild is in labor, so if you can do this yourself, plus trim some of the parts cost, upward of 75 percent of the total cost can be cut.

Overhaul

The actual job of overhaul starts with disassembly of the engine. However, before the engine is torn apart, consideration should be given to the method of cleaning parts. If a cleaning tank is available, all the parts can be dunked for a thorough washing. If not, a steam cleaner will do a good job. If the engine block is to be bored or worked on by a machine shop, the shop will usually include the boiling out as part of the overall price. Otherwise, they will do the job for less than $5. In any case, after the engine is disassembled, each part should be thoroughly cleaned, then any machined surface coated with a light film of oil to prevent corrosion.

Blueprinting

This is the time to decide just how good an engine overhaul is desired. If nothing more than ordinary transportation is necessary, then there is perhaps little call for a super-prepared engine. On the other hand, should you want to create a really smooth-running, dependable power plant, it is wise to consider blueprinting.

Blueprinting is a term used by automotive enthusiasts to designate the process of making an engine mechanically perfect. That is, the many deviations from the original factory specifications—deviations that are sure to crop up during mass production—are removed. The published specifications will call for a certain combustion chamber volume, valve timing, working-part clearances, ignition settings, etc. Passenger-car engines never actually meet these requirements, except in the case of very high-performance (and expensive) street vehicles, such as Chrysler's Street Hemi and Chevrolet's hottest Corvette. In many cases, the mass-production engine is very far indeed from the design requirements. Operational smoothness and increased horsepower will be the direct result of blueprinting.

In essence, to blueprint an engine means to very carefully measure each and every functioning part of the engine and modify them to meet published minimums. That is what a champion stock-car racer must do in order to win; his engine must produce maximum power with stock components.

Factory specs may be difficult to obtain on cars older than 1949, but in all cases, a dealer may be able to supply the necessary data. If not, he can supply the proper address in Detroit where the information may be found. In the rare instance where no specifications are available, the next best thing is to balance all related parts of the engine. That is, make the combustion-chamber volumes of all cylinders identical, use shims to get precisely the same valve-spring pressures (open and closed), take time to check each and every crankshaft-bearing area for identical and sufficient clearance, etc.

During blueprinting, pay particular attention to chamber volume, for the factory figure will invariably be less than your engine measures. To check the volume, plug the spark-plug holes in the head with clay and smooth even with the surrounding chamber. Then, using a graduated beaker, pour the chamber full of oil until the liquid is level with the head surface. Do this to each chamber. Then, using the chamber with the *least* volume as a guide, machine work on the head can be undertaken. It will be easiest to mill the head gasket surface until the chamber with the *most* volume is brought to factory specifications. This means the remaining chambers will be under—smaller—than factory requirements. After the head has been milled, each of these smaller chambers is then opened up by grinding the chamber with a rotary file (get the file from your hardware store). The best place to do the grinding, which will be minimal at most, is around the shrouded part of the valve, for both overhead-valve and flathead engines.

Next, make sure all the valve springs are matched for tension (you may want a professiinal mechanic to help you on this, as he will have the proper special tools), using shims from the parts house as necessary. And remember to check each assembled valve unit by opening the valve to recommended height, making sure the spring coils do not bottom on one another and bind.

Still in the valve department, check the valve timing after the camshaft has been installed and connected to the crankshaft via the timing chain and gear. This requires a dial indicator, so again you may want to call on the professional for assistance.

Another vital place to look for wasted horsepower is in the piston-deck height, or the height from the top of the piston to the head surface of the block. Invariably, this will be more than the factory calls for. To be sure of getting the recommended stock compression ratio, you may have to mill the head surface of the block a few thousandths of an inch. It is often wise to mill the block anyway, since older engines will tend to warp with age. If a higher compression than stock is obtained, through either milling the head or installing high-compression pistons, it is more important than ever to match chamber volumes and check deck height.

There are many other places where blueprinting will be necessary, but these are the most important. It is suggested you follow the factory book and check everything.

The Block

The engine block is usually worked on first. When the cylinder-bore taper—the difference between diameters at the bore top and bottom—exceeds 0.020 to

0.030 inch, the block needs boring. Any engine with from 50,000 to 70,000 miles on it will generally need reboring. Oversize piston rings can be purchased for slight overbores, but as a rule it is best to include new pistons when excessive taper is involved. Overboring is one way to improve an engine's power. From the torque and horsepower calculations, it is obvious that any change in the cubic-inch displacement will increase the torque and horsepower curves.

It is common on a noncompetition engine to increase the bore by 0.030 inch over stock, or the current bore reading. However, since this engine will be cared for better than in the past (hopefully, anyway), it is worthwhile to consider a maximum overbore of around 0.125 inch. Some older engines will take a larger bore, but this is considered the safe typical limit. Engines produced after 1960 will not normally take a large overbore owing to the thin-wall block-casting technique now so popular with the factories. Such an engine has a 0.040 inch overbore maximum.

A word of caution. Before any block machine work is undertaken, it is wise to spend an hour very carefully inspecting the block for cracks. While a broken exterior piece may not necessarily ruin an engine block, any internal cracks are sure-fire death blows. Be especially critical of the area around the cylinder bores, top and bottom. Also check around the valve seats of overhead-valve heads, and in flathead engines check the area between the bore and the valve seat. You're looking for minute hairline cracks, little indications of excessive engine-operating temperatures. They are so small as to be normally unnoticeable, but when the engine warms up, these cracks will open and water ends up in the wrong place. Pay attention to this detail particularly on GMC trucks and Chevy 6's, Ford flathead V8's, and older Chrysler 6's. It goes without saying that a used engine block should be inspected before you lay out cash for a purchase.

Pistons

Before the block is bored it is wise to see what kind of pistons will be readily available. Parts-house catalogues will list all possible oversize pistons for your particular engine, along with prices. The larger the overbore, the higher the piston price. At the same time, always look for larger stock pistons that may be available. The 6-cylinder Plymouths made before 1960 had a counterpart in Dodge trucks, but the truck engines normally had a bigger bore (as well as a much better crankshaft). This same relationship between truck and passenger-car engines exists in early Chevrolets, as well as with Fords. If such a factory replacement stock overbore piston is available, chances are the price will be quite low. Incidentally, if you have an engine whose pistons are virtually impossible to duplicate through local parts suppliers, you can get a complete selection from the Jahn's Piston Company in Los Angeles, California. This company has molds for all cars dating back to before 1900, and advertises in many auto-enthusiast publications.

If special pistons must be ordered, here is another place where additional horsepower can be gained for the engine. The compression ratio also affects power, so replacement pistons available through the parts store generally offer an optional higher compression ratio. Cars made before 1955 had ratios of 8.5 to 1 or less, but gasoline refinements have been such that the modern engine may run as high as 11 to 1 without difficulty. You can raise the compression ratio of any old engine at least one full point and not affect dependability. If the engine has a really low compression ratio, something down around 6 to 1, the ratio can be increased to at least 8.5 to 1.

Boring

When an engine block is bored, the final bore diameter is matched to the pistons to be used. This is very import. An additional few thousandths of an inch are included, and the final clearance is cut away during the honing operation. On the subject of clearances, it is possible to leave much more clearance on an engine today than a few years ago, simply because of better materials and lubricants. Whenever clearance is increased, friction decreases with a resultant longer engine life. Always follow the book when setting piston clearances, which may specify anything from 0.006 to 0.012 inch. The piston manufacturer will indicate a minimum clearance that has been selected to provide maximum product life. However, if you select a top-quality piston ring, it is possible to increase this clearance by 0.002 to 0.004 inch, thereby getting a much freer-running assembly.

As noted, the final clearance is made with the honing operation, so be sure and include this distance in your boring calculations. Honing should be done with a fine-grit stone if soft iron piston rings are used, the type of ring usually preferred for street-driven cars. Hard-surface rings, such as the chrome units, demand a coarser honing stone to insure seating. During the hone cuts, the pattern should be cross-hatched at about a 45-degree angle, which can be achieved by lowering and raising the hone drill at a constant rate.

After the block has been bored, and if no other machining operations are necessary, it should be very carefully and thoroughly cleaned, first with solvent, then with warm water and detergent soap suds. Blow all areas clean with air. All oil-transfer galleries must be cleaned with a small round wire brush and blown clear (this is where the amateur mechanic usually cuts a corner and ends up in trouble); then the machined surfaces should be coated with a film of oil.

To reduce future buildup of oil sludge, the internal area not machined—valve lifter valley, crankcase hollow, etc.—may be painted with Rust-O-Leum. The outside of the block should be painted with a thin coat of heat-resistant engine enamel.

Although block alignment boring is not absolutely

essential, it is an excellent procedure to insure a perfect rebuild. Every time an engine is assembled and run, the various surfaces are under extreme pressures and will distort slightly. For this reason, the crankshaft and camshaft bores will tend to misalign slightly. This alignment will not change drastically enough to completely ruin an overhaul job, but it is there. If you have access to an alignment boring machine (common in school shops), the extra time spent on this phase of block preparation will pay off later. It involves bolting the main bearing caps in place at the correct torque, then running the boring bar through the crankshaft saddle. The same is followed for the camshaft bore. While desirable, alignment boring is not essential to an overhaul.

After the block has been cleaned, the soft plugs may be replaced by either the ordinary drive-in types or the newer bolt-in designs. Whatever soft-plug design is used, make sure the seating area is perfectly clean and liberally coated with a sealing compound. Replacing a leaky soft plug after the engine is in the car is a difficult job.

Crankshaft

The crankshaft must also be given the machine-shop treatment and may require anything from a micropolish to a journal resizing. The individual throws can be turned down to different diameters—that is, one journal may be made smaller than the rest—but this is not a sound practice. It is better to cut all connecting-rod journals to a common undersize, such as minus 0.010 inch, with the same undersizing of the main journals if necessary.

It is possible for a crankshaft to become bent while in use. Always chuck the crankshaft in a lathe and dial indicate each main bearing surface for runout. If the shaft is bent, it may be straightened in a hydraulic press.

A hard-chromed crankshaft is a luxury, but in some engines it is almost a necessity. Take the pre-1960 Plymouth 6. Known by enthusiasts as the flat-crank special, the crankshaft was too soft and thus prone to early failure. Replacing it with a harder Dodge truck shaft is the easiest solution, but for approximately $25 the stock journals can be plated. This is expensive, to be sure, but necessary for the life of the soft crankshaft. To determine whether your old engine shaft had a tendency to fail for this reason, consult an older professional mechanic. Generally, all V8 crankshafts are strong enough for normal use.

Clearances on the crank are determined at this time. If the shaft must be turned undersize, always get the bearings of the desired size first. Place the bearings in a connecting rod with the rod cap torqued in place, then check the diameter with an inside micrometer. Double checking every step insures against making a costly mistake. Most stock engines call for a connecting-rod clearance of 0.002 to 0.0025 inch. Again, this is designated for maximum longevity under abnormal conditions. Since you're going to take care of this engine, you can open up the crank clearances. Bring the rod clearances out to 0.003 inch, duplicate this figure at the mains, and slightly increase rod end play.

This rod side clearance is where many an engine rebuilding goes astray. As the engine friction increases, the metal rods will tend to expand slightly. This closes the distance between the edge of the rods and the crank journal cheek. As this distance is reduced, lubricating oil cannot flow as well, leading to higher temperatures, which lead to greater metal expansion, etc. It's a vicious cycle that must be avoided at all costs. As a guide, since your engine will probably rev up several hundred rpm better than a stock engine, this rod end play must be increased by at least 0.001 inch total. This is done at the same time the journals are ground for diameter, by grinding the cheeks.

Still another neat way to insure maximum engine life through reduced crankshaft friction is to groove the main bearing journals. These grooves may run the journal circumference, being about ⅛-inch wide and ⅟₃₂- to ⅛-inch deep, or they may just extend ½-inch on either side of the oil-delivery holes. The grooves will increase the flow of vital oil.

This oil flow is further facilitated by chamfering the oil-galley holes in both main and rod journals. When the sharp oil-hole edge is removed, the oil can spread through the bearing easier. As this oil flows, it carries away frictional heat, which justifies paying so much attention to the lubrication of the block and crankshaft.

After the journals have been ground, they can be micro-polished to a mirror finish, which reduces bearing wear during break-in.

All oil holes in the crankshaft must be thoroughly cleaned with a wire brush, then washed and blown clear with air. If the amateur does nothing else right on an engine overhaul, he should make sure the oil passages are all clean and clear!

Rods and Bearings

The connecting rods of a stock engine seldom need attention, provided the engine has not been abused or wrecked. As a precaution, however, always check rod alignment. This is one procedure that may best be left to the machine shop, because the big and little rod ends must be measured with an inside micrometer and re-sized if necessary. Rod alignment, or the straightness of the rod, will also be checked and corrected. If your rods are from a very old engine, they may have poured babbit bearings rather than inserts. If such is the case, they must be sent out for repouring, or a new set of replacements must be purchased.

Bearings have a very definite effect upon engine life, so never pay a couple of dollars less and settle for second best. Always buy the best, because bearings in a well-cared-for engine seldom fail. In fact, it is common for 230-mile-per-hour fuel-burning dragster engines to get over 200 runs on a set of bearings, or roughly the equivalent of 150,000 extremely hard miles.

Perhaps the best advice on bearings is to replace the stock type with the tri-metal design, which has evolved during the last decade as the finest for all-around use. Generally speaking, it is better to have a bearing with a soft face, or a face softer than the crankshaft journal. Foreign particles then become imbedded in the bearing surface, and the bearing works as a sort of trap, saving the crankshaft from damage. There is a certain amount of "bearing crush" necessary for a bearing to operate correctly, so follow the manufacturer's installation instructions precisely.

Rings

Each piston-ring groove should be checked for proper ring-to-piston clearance, following the recommendations of the ring maker. Before installing the piston rings, the piston should be assembled to the rod according to individual engine requirements. Some pistons are held in place by snap rings on the pins; others use Teflon buttons; still others use no retainer. In most stock engines, the pin is firmly fitted in the rod. Another trick to get better lubrication is to drill a small hole from the top of the small end of the rod into the bore. Oil splashing around in the crankcase will settle in the hole and lubricate the pin bushing. Of course, this is unnecessary if the engine rods are drilled to get oil under pressure from the crankshaft journal.

Each and every piston ring should be positioned down the cylinder bore at least 1½ inches and parallel to the head surface. The ring end gap is then checked. If this gap is less than the ring manufacturer recommends, it should be increased with a file. Checking the rings will take about five minutes per cylinder, but it is another point of difference between the good and poor mechanic.

The type of ring to use is a matter of personal preference. Chrome rings are excellent in engines scheduled for hard usage, but the same engine will perform just as well with softer rings under normal use. Perhaps better. As a guide, there is no need to get a chrome ring unless the engine has compression over 9.5 to 1, and will be spun over 5500 rpm. At the same time, quality begets quality, so don't cut dollars for cheap rings. Get good ones.

Short Block Assembly

The crankshaft is coated with good assembly lubricant, such as HRL or STP, and dropped in place. Then the main bearing caps are put in place. If you have any doubt about the condition of the main bearing cap bolts, always replace them. The same holds true for rod bolts. After the main caps are torqued down to specifications (a torque wrench is an absolute necessity for engine overhaul), the crankshaft should spin freely in the saddle. If it doesn't, there is misalignment or clearance trouble somewhere, trouble that must be found and corrected.

Next, the piston rings are placed on the pistons; then

each piston is slipped into a cylinder. A ring squeezer will compress the rings so they will slide into the bore. Dip the compressed assembly in oil before actual installation in the block. As a protection for the rod journals, slip a piece of rubber hose over the connecting rod bolts. The piston is then driven into the bore with the handle of a sturdy hammer, using gentle taps. If there is the slightest indication of a bind, stop! It is probably a ring hanging on the top of the cylinder bore, and if the piston is tapped too hard, the ring may be chipped or broken. Tightening the ring squeezer further should solve the problem.

Guide each connecting rod onto the crankshaft carefully, after the insert bearings have been installed on the crank, then bolt on the appropriate rod cap. Note that these caps are marked in some manner to correspond with the rods, and they should not be mismatched between rods or set on the rod backward. After all the rods are in place, torque to specifications. Again, if everything is installed correctly the crankshaft can be rotated, although ring drag will cause movement to be stiff.

The stock oil pump should be replaced if there is any sign of wear on the pump gears or gear-support surfaces. If available, a heavy-duty oil pump should be substituted, as most old pumps were of poor quality. As before, the truck engine is a good place to look for an option. The oil-pump pressure-relief spring can be shimmed or stretched to increase the oil pressure, but this increase should never be more than 20 pounds above stock. Oil pressure does not take the place of increased capacity available through a better pump. Prime the pump with oil before installing it in the block.

It is possible you may want to increase the oil-pan capacity. Nothing wrong with this, and it is easily done by welding an extra sump area in the pan. At the same time, all this oil sloshing around in the sump may be kept near the oil-pump pickup by welding baffles in the pan. When front and rear main bearing seals are installed in the bearing caps and block, always leave a slight bit of gasket material above the surface for positive seal. And when the oil-pan gaskets are installed, coat the surfaces with grease or nonhardening sealant for an extra-good pan seal. This will keep oil from dripping onto the driveway later.

The Camshaft

If the stock camshaft is to be used, it should be carefully inspected for lobe and bearing journal wear. If there is wear, and there most likely will be in an engine with more than 60,000 miles or in an engine with high valve-spring pressures, a new or reground camshaft is necessary. There is no way of getting around this requirement. Some power gain can be bolted into the engine with a different camshaft, but for a good all-around street machine, it is not advisable to install a racing cam. Instead, check with the local dealer and utilize a factory camshaft with a better timing pattern.

Again, the truck version is often the answer, and often a later model engine cam will fit the earlier engine. The cam bearings should always be replaced. A new set of lifters (especially hydraulics) may be required, but since they will be expensive, use the old lifters unless they are absolutely ruined.

Valves

If the engine has the valves in the block, as many older designs do, the valve surfaces must be ground during the block-preparation stage. Otherwise, as with the valve-in-head engine, this can come later. In either case, the valve seats must be ground with a special tool, which may be rented. The valves themselves may or may not be in reusable condition. Save them if you can, because of expense. Check the valve for a bent stem or burned face, then grind the face to the prescribed angle. The valves should be lapped to the seats with lapping compound (this is a hand operation), and if the valves use stem seals, new seals should be installed.

In the case of a valve-in-block engine, the valve-to-head clearance must be checked if a high-compression head (or a planed head) is used, or if a different-lift camshaft has been installed. Place clay strips on the head directly above the valve area, torque the head in place, and rotate the engine several times. Check the thickness of the squashed clay. If it is less than 0.060 inch, additional clearance for the valves must be flycut into the head. A similar clearance check must be made on overhead-valve engines when different cams or pistons are used.

Heads

Heads seldom fail on a car, except for damage due to coolant freezing. Even then, it is possible to repair such a broken head by careful welding, since the break is usually on the outside of the casting.

As with the block overbore, there is a maximum limit to head milling (also called shaving, grinding, and planing). This figure is usually 0.125 inch and should not be exceeded. Whatever cut is made on the head will have a direct effect on the compression ratio, and in turn the valve-to-head clearance. In the case of an overhead-valve engine, when the heads are milled, the intake manifold must be also milled to realign the intake ports.

On any engine, new or old, always check the surface of the head with a straight edge to determine if there is any warpage. Slight warpage must be expected and may be straightened by a clean-up cut, which usually will not change the compression ratio radically. On flathead engines, such warpage may be excessive, however, and in that case, a new head is dictated. Always clean the head and valve assemblies (rockers, shafts, etc.) and coat with a light oil before installation. The head(s) should be installed and torqued down according to specifications, following the alternating torquing

Major parts of Chevrolet V8 overhead-valve engine. Overhaul entails putting parts in proper relationship with correct clearances.

Left: Be careful when installing new camshaft bearings and camshaft. Coat all machined surfaces with assembly lubricant. *Right:* Clean all oil-transfer holes in crankshaft with stainless-steel wire brush, then blow holes clear with air.

Top Left: Plasti-Gage, available from parts stores, is used to check bearing clearance. *Top Right:* Use a torque wrench on all parts of the engine, following the engine manufacturer's specifications exactly. *Bottom Left:* Connecting rods are checked for alignment and twist. They must be straightened if bent. *Bottom Right:* Each piston ring must be inserted squarely in bore. The end gap is measured with a feeler guage.

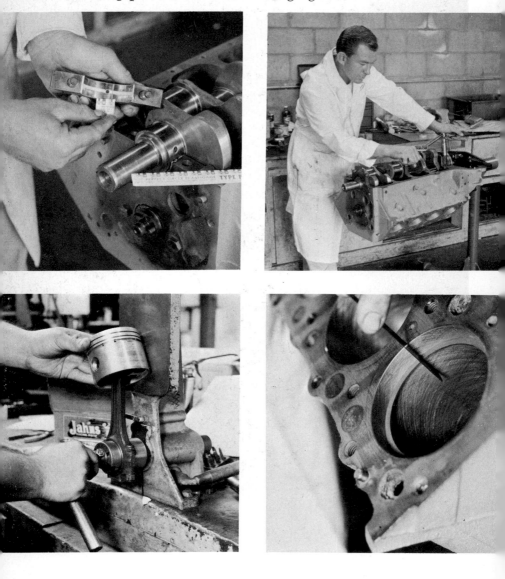

Check individual ring grooves in piston for correct ring clearance. Install rings with correct expander tool.

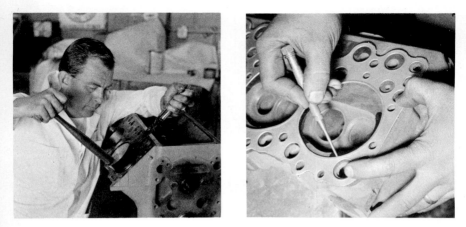

Above Left: Use ring squeezer to compress rings on piston. Tap the assembly into the cylinder bore with a hammer handle. *Above Right:* When blueprinting combustion chambers, scribe head gasket outline as shown. Do not grind outside these limits.

Check connecting-rod side play with feeler guage. Grind crank journal sides or turn down big end of rod for additional clearance.

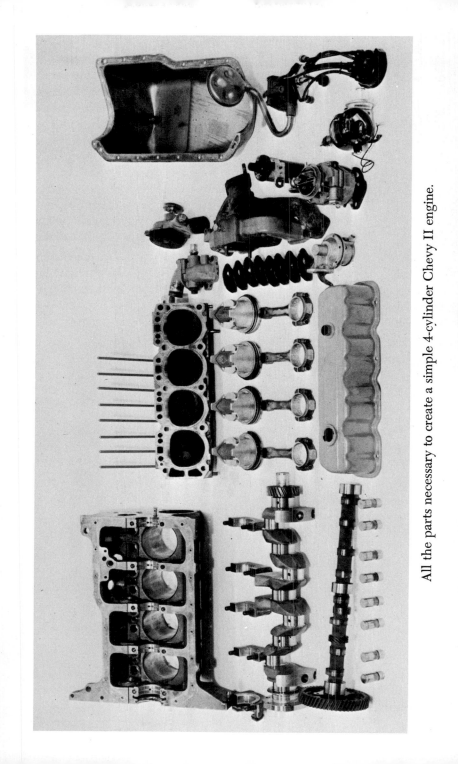

All the parts necessary to create a simple 4-cylinder Chevy II engine.

Above: The Chevrolet V8 engine is powerful and small, works well in all engine swaps where space is a basic problem.

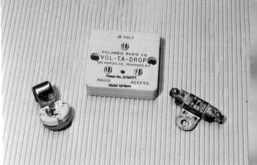

Right: When an engine with a 12-volt electrical system is fitted into a car with a 6-volt system, electrical resistors must be installed.

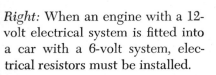

Buick V8 engine is good for swaps because it is narrow.

Left: Chrysler Hemi engine at left can be shoehorned into space normally occupied by Ford flathead, but a smaller engine would be better.

Special dual-point conversion kits, available from most distributors, provide a definite performance advantage.

Tune-up kits such as the IECO unit shown below include new spark-plug wires, spark plugs, and a carburetor repair kit.

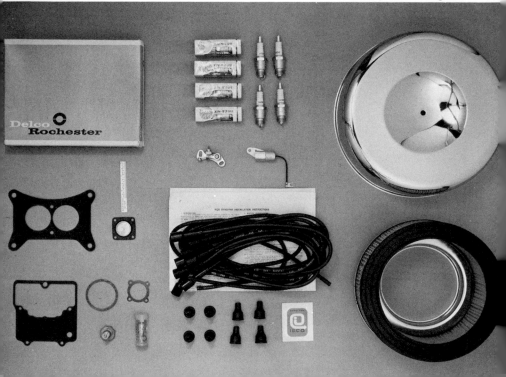

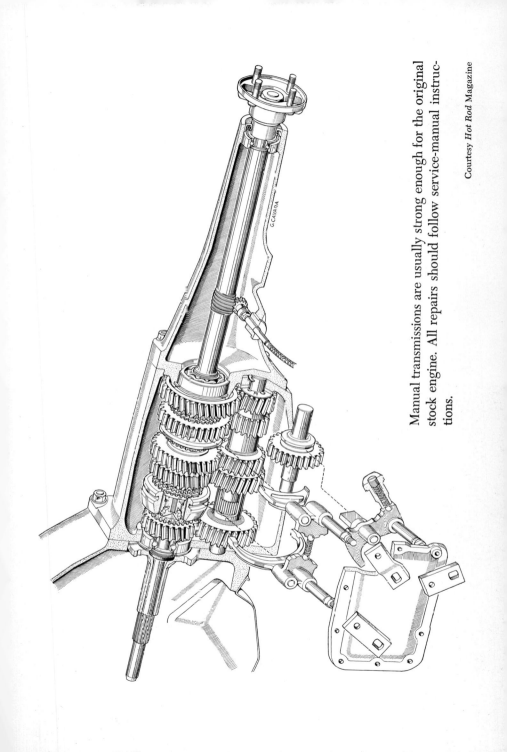

Manual transmissions are usually strong enough for the original stock engine. All repairs should follow service-manual instructions.

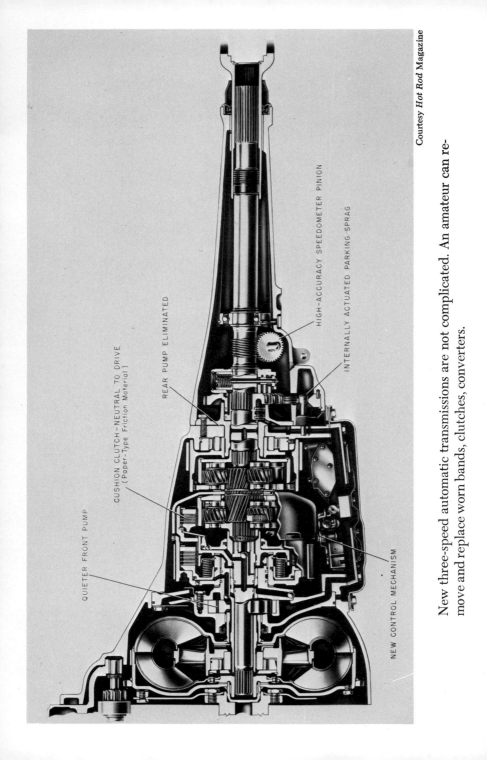

QUIETER FRONT PUMP

CUSHION CLUTCH - NEUTRAL TO DRIVE
(Paper-Type Friction Material)

REAR PUMP ELIMINATED

HIGH-ACCURACY SPEEDOMETER PINION

INTERNALLY ACTUATED PARKING-SPRAG

NEW CONTROL MECHANISM

New three-speed automatic transmissions are not complicated. An amateur can remove and replace worn bands, clutches, converters.

Clutch and disc assembly may be removed and replaced as necessary. New units are usually less expensive than repair.

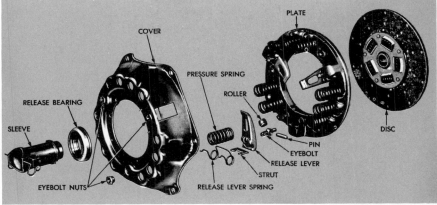

Exploded view of clutch assembly.

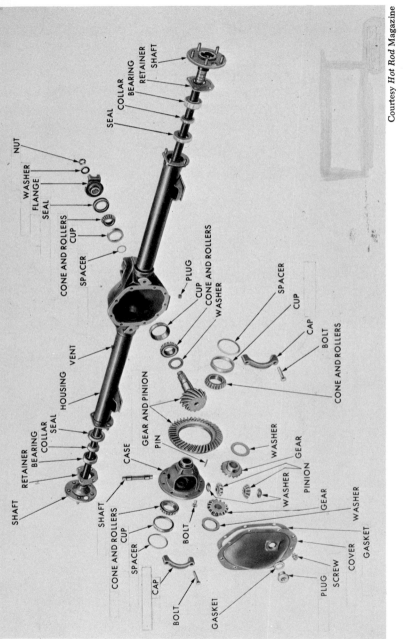

Exploded view of typical rear-end assembly. Setting pinion-gear clearances should be left to a professional.

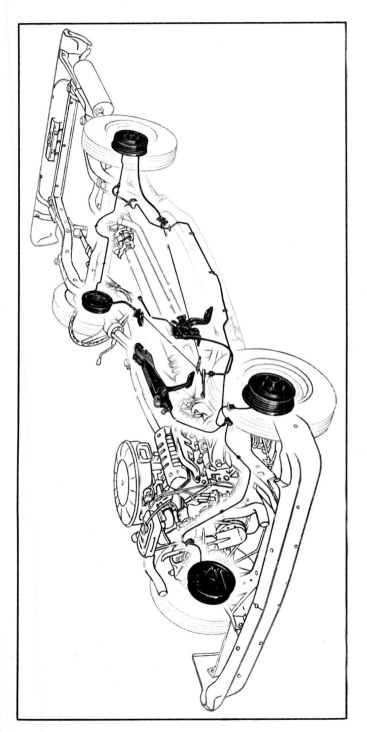

Typical components of a hydraulic brake system.

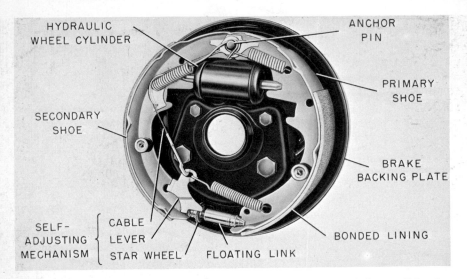

HYDRAULIC WHEEL CYLINDER

ANCHOR PIN

PRIMARY SHOE

SECONDARY SHOE

BRAKE BACKING PLATE

SELF-ADJUSTING MECHANISM { CABLE LEVER STAR WHEEL

FLOATING LINK

BONDED LINING

Modern duo-servo brake with self-adjusting mechanism. "Floating" brake shoes assist in applying brake force.

Single-servo hydraulic brake. Only front shoe helps apply force, typical of 1939–48 Ford cars.

Above: Homemade independent rear end for a 1914 Model T was made from Chevrolet rear end. Coilshock type of springing is common in race cars.

Above Right: Any sign of fluid leakage is an indication that wheel cylinder should be repaired or replaced.

Unit construction, popular with many modern car builders, allows body to take up much of the original frame loads.

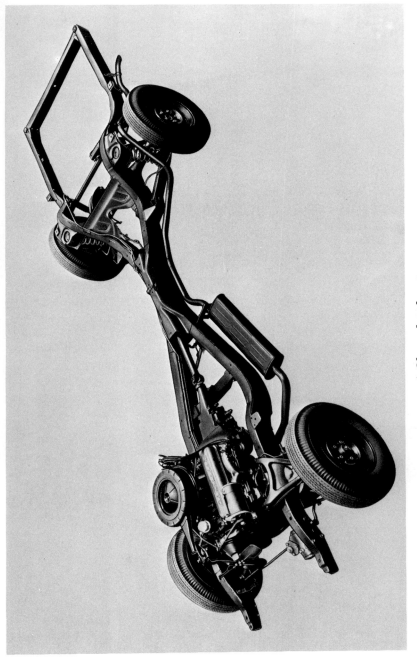

A Chevrolet chassis.

pattern prescribed. After the engine has run for several miles, the headbolts should be retorqued.

Accessories

Fixing up the carburetor and ignition system is covered in the tune-up discussion (Chapter 5), and must not be overlooked during a major overhaul. Nothing will darken enthusiasm so much as a poorly set up distributor, and an incorrectly adjusted carburetor is murder on rings.

It is almost a surety that both generator and starter will need rebuilding. Fortunately, almost every malfunction of either may be fixed at home, short of turning the armature or commutator. A bad end bearing or bushing may allow the armature to sag and drag, but that is easy to fix. Replace the brushes if they are worn more than half their original length, and always have the electrical shop check the wiring for shorts. A new engine is usually tight, so a booster battery will probably be required for the initial one or two starts. If the engine remains tight after that, you didn't check for clearance or misalignment trouble back at the short block assembly stage.

Using the Engine

Breaking in a new engine is a matter of personal habit, but as a rule the first several hundred miles should be driven at reduced speed, with a 50-mile-per-hour maximum. Occasional short bursts to 60 to 70 miles per hour will help the rings seat better, but keep these speed spurts short. After 500 miles, change the oil and filter and drive normally. If the engine has been carefully rebuilt, and if the rings have seated properly, the engine will be good for many thousands of trouble-free miles. There is no reason a rebuilt engine won't top 150,000 miles if it has been carefully assembled, has received new or good used parts, gets proper periodic maintenance, and is not thrashed to death by an overanxious throttle foot.

4 Engine Swaps

Sooner or later, anyone fixing up an old car will get around to the question of engine swaps. What kind of engine will fit into what kind of car? How much trouble will the swap be to make? Where can special parts be bought for improvements? Invariably, the fellow who fixes up a 1950 Ford soon finds the response of the stock engine poor by modern standards. Fortunately, tremendous advances in engine design during the past two decades have resulted in engineering refinements rather than significant overall size increases. In fact, the trend has been to smaller and smaller outside dimensions while power output has sharply increased.

Because the outside measurements of the modern engine—whether a V8, in-line 6, or in-line 4—are so compact, it is a simple matter to get high performance from older cars. However, all-out speed is not the main reason a swap should be considered. More important is availability and cost of replacement parts, midrange power, and dependability. Generally speaking, although a big 425-cubic-inch Ford V8 will make a new-model car run along at nearly 120 miles per hour, the same engine will not make an older car go much over 100 miles per hour. The reason lies in the engineering of body and chassis—that is, in streamlining and in the method of getting the raw power to the ground.

Engine swaps can range from putting a flathead Ford V8 into a Model A, to squeezing an overhead camshaft Pontiac 6 into a Mercedes Benz. In all cases, the purpose is to get more flexibility from the engine compartment so the car will accelerate through the lower speeds better (owing to increased torque), or take the high mountains easier, or run smoother at highway cruising speeds. Even owners of pickup campers are interested in swaps for more low-speed lugging power.

It is a long-standing axiom among automotive enthusiasts that you can put any kind of engine in any car, provided you use a big enough hammer. The average person contemplating an engine swap often has the erroneous impression that little or no special work is involved. An engine is an engine, and a car is a car. This is hardly the case. Every engine swap, even between products of the same company, requires special attention. No swap is hard, but they all must be accompanied by planning.

Speed-equipment shops often sell special swap kits for the more popular combinations, such as the Chevy 283 engine in an early Studebaker. These kits usually include just the hard-to-fabricate items, such as front motor mounts and transmission mount. At the same time, a wide variety of engine-to-transmission adapters are available.

Engine Weight

By referring to the engine-weight chart on page 58, it is easy to see that ultimate power has a direct relationship to engine weight. The big powerhouses such as Oldsmobile and Chrysler weigh about 700 pounds. At the other extreme are the little engines, such as Corvair and the aluminum Buick, that tip the scales at under 350 pounds. Between these two figures are the Fords and Chevys so popular as swapping material.

During recent years, engineering has paid off handsomely in lighter engines, particularly in a reduction in weight of the bare engine block. For example, the Oldsmobile 425-cubic-inch engine weighs less than the older Olds 394, highly regarded for sheer brute power but anchor heavy. The weight saving is due primarily to the now commonly used thin-wall casting technique. Block walls are much thinner (and lighter) with no sacrifice in block strength. This development of familiar iron-alloy engine foundations has only one major drawback—the engine bore cannot be increased significantly for either rebuilding or subsequent engine displacement changes.

Of special interest to the prospective engine swapper is the relationship between engine displacement and horsepower. If high horsepower is needed but

Engine Weights

(Weights are approximate, without clutch, flywheel, or bell housing. Displacement is generally the largest offered in stock form; lower displacement versions have comparable weights.)

ENGINE	DISPLACEMENT (cubic inches)	WEIGHT (pounds)
Buick V6	198	370
Buick (aluminum V8)	215	320
Buick	425	640
Cadillac	390	625
Cadillac	429	600
Chevy II 4	153	350
Chevy II 6	194	410
Chevrolet	283/327	540
Chevrolet	409	640
Chrysler	440	670
Chrysler	392	765
Corvair	145	300
De Soto	383	640
De Soto	341	670
Dodge	325	640
Dodge	361	630
Ford Falcon	170	375
Ford	289	460
Ford	292	625
Ford	427	650
Oldsmobile	394	700
Oldsmobile	425	600
Oldsmobile	330	550
Plymouth	318	580
Pontiac Tempest 4	195	470
Pontiac	421	675
Pontiac	389	650
Pontiac	327	580
Rambler	327	600
Studebaker	289	650
Valiant 6	170	450

weight is a problem, look for an engine that provides a compromise. The Chevrolet 283/327, long a favorite, is not the ultimate when you consider the ratio of weight to horsepower/cubic inches.

The 283/327 series Chevy engine can put out as much as 350 or more horsepower, but with ordinary equipment produces closer to 300 or less. Therefore, the little Chevy V8 has a weight of approximately 2 pounds per horsepower/cubic inch. In reality, the ratio is not even this favorable. On the other hand, the Olds 425 is completely capable of well over 400 horsepower. This gives a ratio of 1.4 pounds per horsepower/cubic inch. Since the Olds weighs only 60 pounds more than the Chevy, obviously a good deal of power is gained at a very slight weight increase. This is an important consideration in any engine swap, second only to cost.

Performance of a car can be indicated simply by reading the ratio of overall vehicle weight to horsepower (remember, horsepower is also related to cubic inches). If a racing car of 1000 pounds has an engine with 1000 horsepower, which is not uncommon, then we've grown to expect top speeds of around 190 to 210 miles per hour. Put this same engine in progressively heavier cars and performance falls off rapidly, because the ratio of horsepower to vehicle weight is not so favorable.

Suppose you have a 1952 Chevy sedan with a stock 283 Chevy V8, weighing in at roughly 3400 pounds. Performance of this car is good, especially in the middle speed ranges of 25 to 75 miles per hour, and overall handling is great. The ratio of weight to horsepower is roughly 11:1, approximately that of a current medium-performance new car. Suppose a 765-pound Chrysler early Hemi is used in the car. Now the ratio starts up the ladder, but most important is the effect of the extra pounds on handling. Since most of the added weight falls directly on the front suspension, the car will be more prone to break the rear end loose, nose over in corners, etc. A difference of 100 pounds in the engine compartment is much more important to handling than an additional passenger in the cockpit.

Here's another example of how the weight-to-horsepower ratio affects the 1952 Chevy. The 1949–50 Cadillac V8 engine will lower the ratio to 12:1, and the later Cad engine will get it down to around 10:1, so performance should start comparing to GTO's and Corvettes. Similar results can be obtained when the 327 or 396 Chevrolet engine is dropped into a pre-1955 Chevy chassis.

If the car in question is big and heavy, say approaching 4000 pounds, a difference of 200 pounds in engine weight will not be so noticeable. Any car this heavy is a problem under any condition, requiring much attention to the chassis for handling, so the extra displacement of a heavy Chrysler Hemi or big Olds is desirable. As a general guide to engine weight for swaps, the lower the weight-to-power ratio, the better (engine weight-to-horsepower as well as total car weight-to-horsepower).

What They Measure

Getting the outside dimensions of modern American engines can be difficult for the average person. First, there are few places where these engines are likely to be available in mixed quantity. Second, it is difficult to find an engine out of the car with all equipment still attached.

The first thing a tape measure will reveal is how similar all engines are in height. Width and length may vary as much as 12 inches or more, but from the pan bottom to carburetor base most engines are about 24 inches. Measurements need not include the height to the top of the carburetor. Instead, measure to the top of the intake manifold, or valve cover(s), whichever is higher. For maximum width check from outside to outside of stock exhaust manifolds, and for the bare width measure this distance minus manifolds (which is important if space is critical and special tubing headers are to be constructed). The pan width indicates the general width of the block at the pan mounting surface, an area roughly adjacent to the frame in most swaps, which allows some speculation on steering-gear interference. The length measurement is from the bellhousing face to the fan-pulley face. Always measure to the nearest inch, but if the swap clearance is critical, take closer measurements.

In many cases, romance dictates engine choice for a swap: a Buick engine worked well in the last car, so how about using another one, etc. The successful swapper is concerned only with the most practical conversion. Take the big Buick V8, for instance. Here is a fine engine, with over 400 cubic inches and good low-end torque. It compares in width to the 283/325 Chevy without headers, but in length it presents a problem. It is 33 inches long, about 4 inches longer than the Chevy. This length, due to an extended water-pump shaft, may make the engine too long for a good swap or necessitate extensive pump machine work. Because of the cost of such machine work, the Buick would not be a practical swap where fore-aft engine room is tight.

Engine measurements play a larger role in swaps than is generally understood, for such things as length and height and width are directly related to weight distribution. Here's how it works. The big 390/425 Ford engines make perfect swaps for the early 1955–57 T-Birds. However, the smaller 289 produces a better all-around car. The answer lies in engine length. The big V8 is 24 inches long, but is bulky well forward and therefore has more weight toward the front suspension. The small V8 is only 2 inches shorter, but does not have as much bulk in the water-pump area, thereby reducing front-end weight. Add to this small shift in weight distribution the difference in total engine weight, roughly 200 pounds, and the reason for better handling is apparent.

From the engine-measurements chart on pages 66–68 you can see the similarity among outside engine dimensions. As noted, the problem of clearance is primarily in width and length; height is not so important. For the most part, the smaller cars (Valiant, Dart, Comet, Falcon, American, Chevy II, etc.) will take only the narrower, small V8. The big interference is in suspension, since coil-spring towers are a part of several designs, and the upper A-arms interfere in others. The problem of steering clearance can be overcome with ingenuity, or sometimes by simple tubing headers.

Length can also be taken care of through modifications to the firewall, moving the radiator forward, or both. Still, the less reshaping of body metal necessary, the better.

Adapters are really a part of a "willingness to go in the hole," for they are inherently the result of clearance problems (with the exception of the transmission adapter, of course). For example, the Chevy engine requires no adapters. The starter motor is on the right, with nothing for steering-clearance trouble but a very small oil filter. But where the Chevy engine drops right in most places, the other GM products can be a pain. The Buick and Olds starters are on the left, but may be repositioned by an adapter. Adapters move the fuel pumps, when necessary, and the oil filters may be remotely mounted if they interfere.

Making It Fit

There are all kinds of problems in putting a different engine in a chassis, varying in number and magnitude. If the swap is a popular one, the problems have been solved by others. If not, you're the Lone Ranger. A swap can usually be divided into five problem areas: mechanical, lubrication, cooling, fuel, and electrical. The mechanical part will always seem the greatest problem, but in reality this normally turns out to be the smallest. The incidentals, such as fuel-line and throttle linkage and wiring, distinguish the thorough workman from the sloppy one.

The mechanical aspects of an engine swap are limited to squeezing an engine into an alien compartment. As noted, adapters are available to handle transmission mating, and a number of mount kits are marketed for the popular swaps. There is still much fitting involved, however, which will often require the reshaping of fender splash panels. The splash panel usually is cut to make room for the generator or power-steering pump, so one method of keeping stock panels is to relocate the generator or pump.

In the steering department, there is often a problem of clearance between the oil pan and tie rod, particularly if the oil pan has a front or midpoint sump. Again, the kits for popular swaps have special dropped tie rods and attendant pieces to ease the chore. However, if the swap is not so common, there is a chance of steering-system trouble. It is always wise to limit clearance work to the tie rod, if possible.

The only lubrication problem involved in a swap is the oil filter, and this can be alleviated by using special adapters. Filter block-off plates are available, but it is never advisable to remove a full-flow filter. Put the filter anywhere, but never throw it away!

Cooling is normally not a problem with an engine swap, simply because most late engines are so efficient in cooling that any radiator is effective. Putting an overhead-valve engine into one of the early Fords, cars notorious for running hot with Flathead V8's, usually results in a problem on the other end of the scale—i.e., the engine runs too cool. The Chevy and Olds engines are good choices if you can find a thermostat that will keep the late engines at the proper operating temperature.

The problems of fuel are minor, especially if you use the stock fuel pump. However, if you use an electric fuel pump, remember that these pumps were designed to *push* the gasoline to the engine, not *pull* it. Therefore, an electric pump should be mounted as near the gas tank as possible, not on the firewall!

Most swappers get tangled up in the electrical area. The simplest aproach to this problem is to use the stock wiring harness if at all possible, extending various wires where necessary. The 6-volt wiring will carry 12-volt current easily, so you need change only the minor control features, such as relays and regulators, to 12-volt, as well as all light bulbs and sending units (gas tank and oil pressure, etc.). Special voltage restrictors are available from auto-parts stores if you don't want to change to 12-volt accessories.

Properly done, an engine swap should provide superior performance over the original engine and chassis

Engine Measurements

(outside dimensions in inches)

Engine	Height	Length	Width Maximum	Width Bare	Pan Area	Motor Mounts	Starter	Filter	Pan Sump
American Motors									
V8	22	31	24	22	11	Side-front	Right	Left	Rear
Flathead 6	21	29	15	15	10	Front	Left	Option	Rear
OHV6	26	30	18	15	11	Front	Left	Option	Rear
Chrysler Corporation									
Early Hemi	23	31	29	29	11	Side-front	Left	Right	Rear
Late Hemi	25	30	29	29	10	Side-front	Left	Left	Mid
A series	24	29	28	26	11	Side-front	Left	Right	Mid
B series	24	30	26	23	10	Side-front	Left	Left	Mid
Slant 6	26	30	20	20	9	Middle	Left	Right	Mid
Ford Motor Company									
Small V8 (260–289)	22	28	21	19	9	Middle	Right	Left	Front
Early V8 (292–352)	24	28	28	23	10	Middle	Right	Left	Front
Late (Big) V8 (390–406–427)	24	30	27	23	10	Middle	Right	Left	Front
Small OHV6	20	31	17	17	9	Middle	Right	Left	Front
Big OHV6	27	32	13	13	9	Middle	Right	Right	Front
Flathead V8	22	30	26	26	9	Front	Right	Option	Rear

General Motors

Buick

Straight 8	26	45	14	12	9	Middle	Right	Right	Rear
Small V8	21	28	25	20	8	Middle	Right	Right	Mid
Small V6	22	23	24	20	10	Side-front	Right	Right	Mid
Big V8	24	33	29	22	11	Side-front	Right	Left	Rear

Cadillac

Big V8	23	28	28	25	11	Side-front	Left	Right	Rear

Chevrolet

OHV4	24	24	20	15	10	Side-front	Right	Right	Front
Late OHV6	24	33	16	13	10	Middle	Right	Right	Mid
Early OHV6	26	32	17	14	10	Side-front	Right	Remote	Rear
Small V8 (260–327)	22	28	25	19	6	Side-front	Right	Left	Rear
Medium V8 (409)	22	30	28	25	8	Middle	Right	Left	Rear
Big V8	22	30	28	25	9	Middle	Right	Left	Rear
Corvair	17	29	27	—	—	Rear	Rear	Front	Flat

Oldsmobile

Small V8	21	28	26	25	8	Front	Left	Right	Rear
Medium V8 (330)	22	29	23	22	10	Front	Left	Right	Rear
Big V8 (early)	23	32	30	26	9	Front	Left	Right	Rear
Big V8 (late)	23	29	30	26	9	Front	Left	Right	Rear

Engine Measurements (*Continued*)

(outside dimensions in inches)

Engine	Height	Length	Width Maximum	Width Bare	Pan Area	Motor Mounts	Starter	Filter	Pan Sump
Pontiac									
Slant 4	21	29	17	17	10	Side	Left	Right	Rear
Small V8	21	28	26	25	8	Front	Left	Right	Rear
Medium V8	22	29	23	22	10	Front	Left	Right	Rear
Big V8	24	28	25	23	10	Front	Left	Right	Rear
Flat 6	22	33	21	21	10	Front	Left	Option	Rear
Studebaker									
OHV V8	22	28	26	25	9	Side-front	Left	Option	Rear

Note: All measurements are from bellhousing face to fan-pulley face. Maximum width is with stock headers; bare block width is minus headers. Height is distance from bottom of pan to top of intake manifold (or valve covers). Starter and filter location is as viewed from rear of engine.

combination. There is no reason this will not happen if the swaper has taken time to do each job properly and selected the correct engine in the first place.

Typical Retail Prices of Used OHV V8 Engines

ENGINE	PRICE (Complete Good)	PRICE (Core)
Buick		
All big V8's	$75–$450	$30–$125
Special small V8	$150–$400	$30–$75
Cadillac	$50–$400	$30–$125
Chevrolet		
265	$50–$200	$20–$75
283	$100–$250	$50–$130
327	$175–$350	$85–$175
348	$50–$200	$20–$75
409	$85–$250	$50–$150
427	$350–$550	$125–$200
(new 396 and 427 Chevrolet designs not included due to rarity)		
Chrysler (includes all Chrysler Corporation engines)		
331–392		
241–335 1951–58 Hemi's	$50–$250	$25–$100
276–341		
A series	$75–$250	$25–$90
B series	$75–$250	$40–$100
426 Hemi	(not available yet)	$325
Ford (includes all Ford Company engines)		
239–312	$5–$100	$0–$50
332–428	$200–$400	$75–$150
221–289	$100–$350	$50–$150
Oldsmobile		
303–324	$5–$100	$0–$50
371–394	$15–$150	$10–$50
400–427	$250–$450	$125–$200
330–up (new series)	$225–$400	$50–$125
Pontiac		
287–389	$5–$400	$0–$125
421	$300–$450	$140–$200

5 Tune-up

Few drivers ever know when their automobile is in proper running order. For that matter, the average car is seldom in perfect tune. There is such a latitude in engine performance that only the race driver would ever need pinpoint accuracy. Still, if an engine is kept as near perfect tune as possible, performance will remain consistently good over a very long period of time. The benefits of attention to the tune-up all end in the pocketbook: better mileage and longer engine life.

For the beginning mechanic, the bolts and nuts of fixing up an old car come fairly easy. Making the car run well, or even run at all, is another problem. Too often, an engine rebuilding job may only take two or three days, but the right tune is never achieved. The mysteries of tune-up can all be solved with patience and attention to minor details. *And* a good *motor manual.* A tune-up without the specific car requirements is like a medical check-up without a doctor.

There are three specific and distinct areas involved in tuning up an internal-combustion engine. The same three are also paramount to successful engine trouble-shooting, since troubleshooting is nothing more than a form of tuning. When a car is being tuned for maximum performance (keep in mind that such performance means making any particular engine work at its absolute best efficiency), when a rebuilt engine is being readied to run for the first time, or when trouble-shooting is involved, check these three things in order: Fire, Fuel, and Compression.

Lack of proper ignition causes poor engine performance in the largest percentage of cases, the problem occurring anywhere between the spark-plug points and the battery. Fuel, or lack of it in the correct ratio, is the next culprit. Even so, there is little that can go wrong with a fuel system. Finally, the engine must have compression to run. When this compression is missing, or is too low to produce top power, the last link to performance is broken. Although one of the three phases of engine operation may cause a malfunction independent of the other two, a general tune-up will usually involve at least fire and fuel when the engine has been run less than 50,000 miles since new or last overhauled. Compression problems are usually an indication of an internal mechanical failure, such as broken or worn rings, a burned piston, or burned valves.

When tuning an engine, or troubleshooting, never assume anything. The gas tank *can* be empty. The battery cable *can* be poorly grounded. The cylinder heads *can* be loose. When trying to find a specific fault within any of the three potential problem areas, be thorough and complete. It seems the cause is usually insignificant.

Before making the initial checks of the ignition system, on either a new or used engine, always first check to see if fuel is being delivered to the carburetor throttle bores. If it is, chances are the engine will run reasonably well. Attention can then be turned to the fire.

When making a fire check, first pull the coil second-

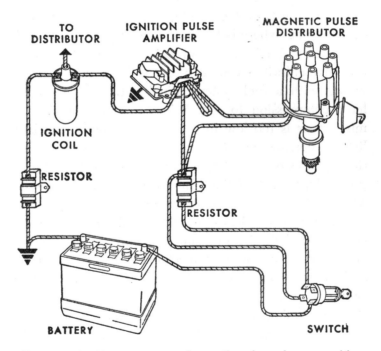

Transistor ignition system can be easily adapted to any older engine and is especially well suited to in-line engines.

ary wire from the distributor cap and see if current is being delivered to the distributor. If it is, remove the spark-plug wire and again check for fire. Hold the wire tip about a quarter inch from any metal surface. If the spark jumps from the wire to the metal, everything is fine. But if the spark jumps from the metal to the wire, the coil polarity is reversed. Reversing the polarity (coil wires wrongly hooked up) is common when an engine is overhauled.

If fire is being delivered to the spark plugs, but the engine is still erratic, particularly under load conditions, the plug itself should be suspected. The plug tip will tell many things about the engine. If the tip is dark and oily (wet), the piston rings may be bad. If the tip is a brownish gray, the engine should be firing properly. If the tip looks burned or overheated, the plug range is too hot. If the tip looks new and wet, the plug range is too cold.

Much more can be learned from the plugs than there is room to explain here. However, auto-parts houses usually stock a handy spark-plug reference guide printed by the plug manufacturers. Check the spark plug on a testing machine if possible; otherwise always replace plugs with a new set of the correct heat range. If the right plug point-gap specifications are not readily available, set the gap at 0.032 inch. This will at least allow the engine to run.

The quality of the spark itself has a very definite bearing on how an engine will run. It is not uncommon for an older car to develop tune problems when either the coil or condenser go bad. In this case, the fire may still reach the spark plug but be too weak to fire the plug under compression. An indication of weak fire is a reddish spark color, rather than a strong blue color.

If fire is being delivered to the distributor but not to the plugs, the trouble is in either the plug wires or the distributor. Plug wires are especially bothersome, since the car may develop an erratic miss at varying engine speeds, with the cause very difficult to trace. (For a guide to plug wires, see Chapter 8 on wiring.) Always install a full set of new secondary wiring if the engine has been driven more than 50,000 to 75,000 miles, or if the car is more than three years old. Often, brand-new cars will have bad secondary wiring.

In the distributor, suspect point trouble first. Points, especially those in older cars, are critical to engine performance. Never try to save a set of points, unless in an emergency. Always install new points and condensers as a set, being careful not to disturb any of the internal distributor wiring. With the points installed, rotate the engine until the points are open widest, then set the gap to specifications. If no specs are handy, set an in-line engine at 0.018 inch, a V8 at 0.015 inch. If the points are ever filed to remove pits and ridges, do so very carefully, and then only with a genuine point file. Never use emery paper or a fingernail file. In an emergency, ordinary writing paper is abrasive enough to clean the points.

Check inside the distributor cap for signs of spark

arcing and carbon paths. If the cap is cracked, or carbon has made a streak in the cap, replacement is usually necessary. Clean each secondary wire plug hole, and clean the cap with a lint-free rag. The distributor rotor can also be cracked or plagued by carbon tracks. A little-known rotor problem is sloppiness caused by an enlarged shaft-locating slot. If this occurs, the rotor can work from side to side and cause erratic performance.

It is always wise to have the distributor set up on an ignition machine if possible. If one is available, its use is simple and easily learned. If the job is farmed out to a professional, the cost is minimal. After a distributor has been removed from the engine, setting the timing back at the correct point is often difficult and frustrating. In fact, setting timing close enough to make a newly rebuilt engine start and run plagues even experienced car enthusiasts.

It is common for the amateur mechanic to set the distributor 180 degrees out of time. When this occurs, the engine will turn over on the starter easily, but has a noticeable tendency to fire back through the carburetor. Of course, the same firing back is common to a distributor retarded too far. To set the distributor for initial running, pull the number-one spark plug, then rotate the engine until that piston is on the compression stroke (felt by keeping the finger over the plug hole). Watch the timing mark on the crankshaft pulley and place it on the zero mark, then just barely break the distributor points by slightly rotating the distributor body. Tighten the distributor hold-down bolt, and put the plug wires in the cap according to the firing order, with the number-one wire nearest the rotor tip.

Of course, the timing should be set according to specifications, but can be set very closely by road testing. If the timing is slow, the engine may heat up and response will be sluggish. Slowly advance the distributor until a slight ping can be heard when the throttle is suddenly opened with the car in high gear and running at 30 miles per hour. When this slight ping is heard, retard the distributor just a bit until the ping disappears. This setting will be close to perfect.

Keep in mind that much fire trouble can be caused elsewhere in the hot wiring circuit. Make sure there is a voltage restrictor in the lead ahead of the coil if the car requires one (most do); otherwise the coil can be burned out by too much voltage. Above all, make sure that the battery is well grounded and that there is a good ground strap between the engine and frame if the battery ground does not connect directly to the frame.

Fuel trouble develops from either an impurity in the gasoline or a mechanical malfunction (a part does wear out). As for contamination of the gas, dirt is usually trapped in the fuel filter but may pass on to the carburetor and become trapped in the float bowl or one of the many small openings. Gums, which can be trapped in the gasoline, may plug up the carburetor, but this is not common. Water is common, more so in the colder climates. The only cure for gas contamination is to clean the gas tank and gas line.

The fuel pump will wear out. In such a case, it is wise to replace it with a new pump, not a rebuilt one. The carburetor will not normally wear out or break unless the throttle shaft wears in the housing. If the shaft is too loose, a new carburetor, or at least a new base, is essential.

Whenever an extensive tune-up is contemplated, plan on cleaning the carburetor and installing a repair kit. Kits for older cars are inexpensive, and installation is quick and easy. Unless the carburetor is very complicated—for example, a modern four-barrel carb—it can usually be reassembled without reference to a manual. However, getting the float level exact is imperative. If the float is set too high, the mixture will be too rich. Too low, and the mixture will be lean, which shows up on corners when the engine seems to stagger momentarily as though out of gas.

Auto-parts stores sell pints and quarts of carburetor cleaner, so a boil-out can be done at home economically. After the boiling process, wash the parts with water and blow dry with air. Never put gaskets or rubber parts in the cleaning solution, which will destroy them. After the carb is reassembled, screw the idle bleed adjustment(s) all the way in (these are in the base of the housing, below the throttle butterflies), then back them out one and a half turns. For the most part, older cars should idle smoothly at around 500 to 600 rpm. If after the carburetor overhaul the engine doesn't accelerate well when coming off idle, lengthen the accelerator pump stroke. On some old carburetors,

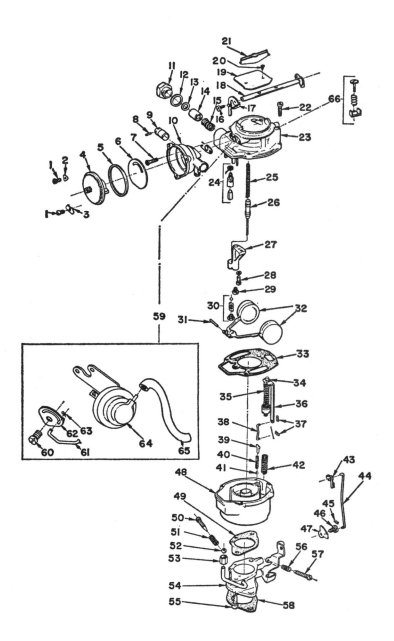

Exploded view of typical Rochester single-throat carburetor.

1. Screw—Stat Cover
2. Retainer—Plain
3. Retainer—Toothed
4. Stat Cover & Coil Assembly
5. Gasket—Stat Cover
6. Baffle Plate
7. Screw—Choke Housing
8. Pin—Choke Piston
9. Choke Piston
10. Choke Housing
11. Fitting—Fuel Inlet
12. Gasket—Fuel Inlet
13. Gasket—Fuel Inlet Filter
14. Fuel Filter
15. Spring—Fuel Filter
16. Screw—Choke Lever
17. Piston Lever & Link Assembly
18. Choke Shaft Assembly
19. Choke Valve
20. Screw—Choke Valve
21. Support—Air Cleaner
22. Screw—Air Horn
23. Air Horn Assembly
24. Needle and Seat Assembly
25. Spring—Power Piston
26. Piston—Power
27. Support—Main Well
28. Screw—Main Well Support
29. Main Metering Jet
30. Power Valve Assembly
31. Pin—Float Hinge
32. Float Assembly
33. Gasket—Air Horn
34. Retainer—Pump Assembly

35. Spring—Pump Duration
36. Pump Plunger Assembly
37. Retainer Pin
38. Link—Pump
39. Guide—Pump Discharge
40. Spring—Pump Discharge
41. Ball—Pump Discharge
42. Spring—Pump Return
43. Clip—Choke Rod
44. Choke Rod
45. Pin—Choke Rod
46. Screw—Cam Attaching
47. Cam—Fast Idle
48. Float Bowl Assembly
49. Gasket—Throttle Body
50. Idle Needle
51. Spring—Idle Needle
52. Packing—Choke Tube
53. Nut—Choke Tube
54. Throttle Body Assembly
55. Screw—Throttle Body
56. Spring—Idle Stop Screw
57. Screw—Idle Stop
58. Gasket—Throttle Body
59. Vacuum Break Diaphragm Assembly
    (Model BV)
60. Screw
61. Link
62. Lever—Choke Shaft
63. Retainer Pin
64. Vacuum Break Assembly
65. Hose—Vacuum
66. Idle Vent Valve Assembly

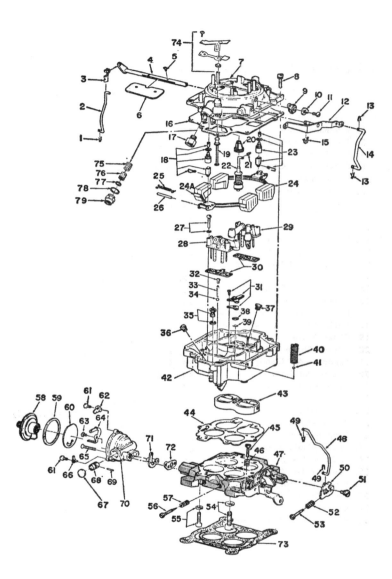

Exploded view of typical four-barrel carburetor.

1. Clip—Intermediate Choke Rod (lower)
2. Intermediate Choke Rod
3. Clip—Intermediate Choke Rod (upper)
4. Choke Shaft and Lever Assembly
5. Screw—Choke Valve
6. Choke Valve
7. Air Horn Assembly
8. Screw—Air Horn
9. Choke Lever and Collar Assembly
10. Choke Trip Lever
11. Screw—Choke Trip Lever
12. Pump Shaft and Lever Assembly
13. Clip—Pump Rod
14. Pump Rod
15. Clip—Pump Shaft and Lever
16. Gasket—Air Horn
17. Fuel Inlet Fitting
18. Needle and Seat Assembly (primary)
19. Power Piston Assembly
20. Boot—Pump Plunger
21. Clip—Pump Plunger
22. Pump Plunger Assembly
23. Needle and Seat Assembly (secondary)
24. & 24A. Float Assembly
25. Float Balance Spring and Clip Assy.
26. Float Hinge Pin
27. Venturi Cluster Screw and Lockwasher
28. Venturi Cluster (primary)
29. Venturi Cluster (secondary)
30. Gaskets—Venturi Cluster
31. Idle Compensator Assembly
32. Guide—Pump Discharge
33. Spring—Pump Discharge
34. Check Ball—Pump Discharge
35. Power Valve Assembly
36. Main Metering Jet (primary)
37. Main Metering Jet (secondary)
38. Pump Inlet Screen Retainer
39. Pump Inlet Screen
40. Spring—Pump Return
41. Check Ball—Pump Inlet
42. Float Bowl Assembly
43. Auxiliary Throttle Valve Assembly
44. Gasket—Throttle Body to Bowl
45. Screw—Idle Speed
46. Spring—Idle Speed Screw
47. Throttle Body Assembly
48. Choke Rod
49. Clips—Choke Rod Attaching
50. Fast Idle Cam
51. Screw—Fast Idle Cam
52. Spring—Fast Idle Screw
53. Fast Idle Screw
54. Screw—Throttle Body to Bowl (large)
55. Screw—Throttle Body to Bowl (small)
56. Idle Mixture Screw
57. Spring—Idle Mixture Screw
58. Choke Cover and Coil Assembly
59. Gasket—Choke Cover and Coil
60. Choke Baffle Plate
61. Screws—Choke Cover Attaching
62. Retainers—Choke Cover (toothed)
63. Screw—Choke Piston Lever
64. Choke Piston Lever and Link Assembly
65. Screw—Choke Housing Attaching
66. Retainer—Choke Cover
67. Plug—Choke Housing
68. Choke Piston
69. Pin—Choke Piston
70. Choke Housing Assembly
71. Intermediate Choke Shaft and Lever
72. Gasket—Choke Housing
73. Gasket—Carburetor to Manifold
74. Idle Vent Valve Assembly
75. Spring—Filter Element Relief
76. Filter Element
77. Gasket—Filter Element
78. Gasket—Fuel Inlet Fitting
79. Fuel Inlet Fitting

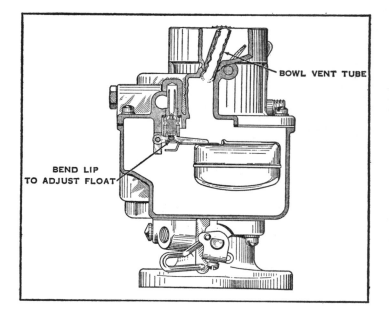

Relationship of float to bowl and needle valve in Carter single-throat carburetor. Float level must be set perfectly.

there are special adjustment holes in the linkage; on others the connecting arm must be bent.

The final part of any tune-up is mainly a mechanical diagnosis. If, after tuning an engine, it still runs poorly, suspect an internal problem. Check individual cylinder compression with a gauge. If any cylinder is more than 15 or 20 pounds below the average, it probably has the mechanical ill, which will be a blown head gasket, burned piston, broken ring, or bad valves.

For a quick check of cylinder condition, especially when the engine seems to have a definite miss, ground

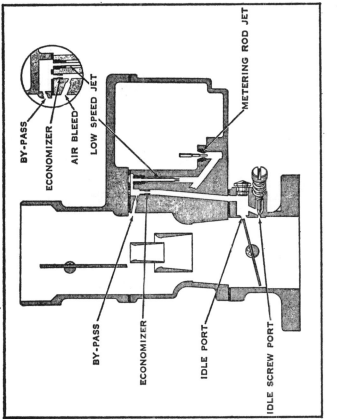

When car runs poorly at idle, idle circuit of carburetor is probably gummed and must be boiled out.

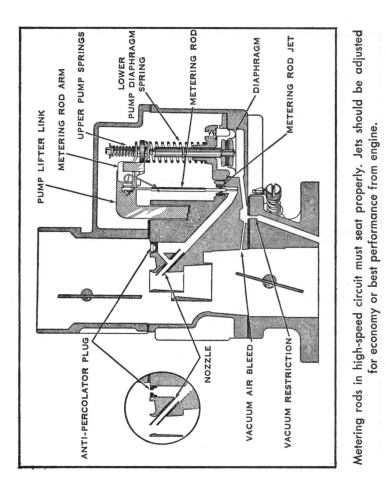

PUMP LIFTER LINK

METERING ROD ARM

UPPER PUMP SPRINGS

LOWER
PUMP DIAPHRAGM
SPRING

METERING ROD

DIAPHRAGM

METERING ROD JET

ANTI-PERCOLATOR PLUG

NOZZLE

VACUUM AIR BLEED

VACUUM RESTRICTION

Metering rods in high-speed circuit must seat properly. Jets should be adjusted for economy or best performance from engine.

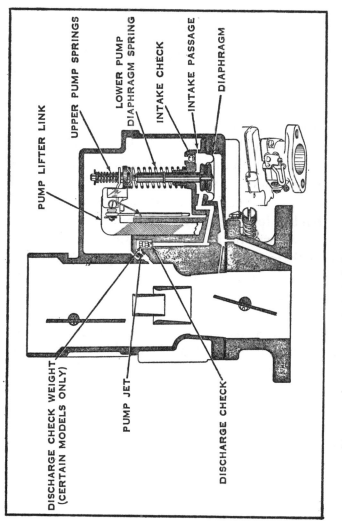

DISCHARGE CHECK WEIGHT (CERTAIN MODELS ONLY)

PUMP LIFTER LINK

UPPER PUMP SPRINGS

LOWER PUMP DIAPHRAGM SPRING

INTAKE CHECK

INTAKE PASSAGE

DIAPHRAGM

PUMP JET

DISCHARGE CHECK

New accelerator pump is included in every carburetor repair kit.

each plug wire (or remove it from the plug) in succession. When the bad cylinder is found, removing or grounding the plug wire will not affect how the engine runs. Removing the wire from a good cylinder will create a definite miss.

A rough idle can often be traced to poor combustion. A burned (or, more common, bent) intake valve will produce a rough idle and tendency to fire back through the carburetor. A burned exhaust valve, which is very common on older cars, will give an emphatic loss of power and strong engine miss. Burned pistons and bad rings tend to foul the spark plugs. Sometimes a blown head gasket will be indicated by water on the spark plug. If there is an indication of compression trouble, always check the valve lash clearance first. One of the valves may be too tight, allowing it to remain open and thus lose compression.

Finally, check for an erratic idle by tightening the intake manifold bolts. Manifold trouble can occur on V8's, but is more common on in-line engines, where the intake manifold can be misaligned as little as an eighth of an inch and let extra air into the ports. A quick check of this can be made by squirting oil around the manifold mating surface. If the oil disappears, you have a leak.

Remember, tune-up and troubleshooting go hand in hand. Check fire first, then fuel, finally compression. And never assume that anything is all right, not even the smallest electrical wiring connection or vacuum hose.

6 Transmissions and Rear Ends

Old car transmissions and rear ends have a way of going bad and staying that way, unless the proper repair and maintenance are observed. Of all the mechanical ailments of the older automobile, a problem in either of these areas is usually most destructive. The old engine may be repaired time and again, but when the gearbox or axles break, the junkpile is just around the corner. It needn't be.

A person does not need a background in mechanical engineering to fix a transmission or limited-slip differential. In virtually every case, it is just a matter of replacing bad parts. But unlike the engine, these units are more complex for the amateur, so a good repair manual is an invaluable partner.

Transmissions

A transmission is necessary in the automobile because the internal-combustion engine does not generate great torque (twisting motion) at low rpm. Some kind of mechanical advantage, or leverage, must be built into the power train to allow the engine to operate efficiently. The transmission provides this leverage. By multiplying the low torque of an engine at near idle speeds, the car can be moved without stalling the engine. The ideal transmission would allow the engine to operate at maximum torque constantly, with the transmission infinitely variable to compensate for differing speed requirements. So far, no one has invented such a gearbox. Nevertheless, both the manual and automatic transmissions of cars built after 1920 do an excellent job.

Standard Transmissions

Manual transmissions of U.S.-built cars will normally have three forward speeds and one reverse, particularly if the car was made prior to 1960. The four-speed gearbox, which has four forward speeds, did not become widely popular until 1960, and then only as an offshoot of drag racing. The basic difference between the two is simply one extra gear between low and high, effectively cutting down the span between the individual gears. That is, with a four-speed transmission, engine rpm can remain more constant. As an example, consider the diesel truck, which may have upward of twenty forward speeds. The diesel engine must be kept within a very narrow rpm range, so much gear shifting is necessary.

Another difference between three- and four-speed

transmissions is minor, but sometimes significant. Most three-speed transmissions, especially those built before the early 1960's, do not have a synchromesh low gear. All four-speed transmissions are synchromesh equipped.

During the last three decades, considerable improvement has been made in the manual transmission, and an old car can probably be equipped with a much stronger similar-make transmission from a newer car. Mixing internal gears between different makes of transmissions is seldom possible.

All modern manual transmissions—meaning gearboxes made since at least 1928—have essentially the same basic parts. A typical unit will have the housing, or major enclosure for the gears; a tailshaft housing, for the output shaft; and in some instances, a bellhousing integral with the main housing. Until the 1960's, all transmissions were made of cast iron. The only advantage aluminum has for transmission cases is lighter weight.

Extending through the front of the transmission case is a splined input shaft which is rotated by the engine. Extending out the rear of the gearbox is the mainshaft, which connects via a universal joint to the driveshaft. Some tailshaft housings and mainshafts are quite long because a long driveshaft has a tendency to whip out of balance at high rpm. By making the mainshaft longer, driveshaft length can be reduced, thereby cutting down on driveshaft balance problems. Between the input and mainshaft are the gears that make torque multiplication possible.

All the rotating shafts in a transmission are carried by bearings or bushings pressed or locked into the housings. These bearings seldom fail unless the transmission has been run without oil, or the oil has been contaminated. However, always rotate the bearings and check for bind or sloppiness, and replace if necessary.

Maintenance and Repair of Standards

Taking a transmission apart is much like disassembling a kitchen clock: reassembly is easy if you remember exactly how the parts go. This is not too difficult on the older transmissions, or those made from 1930 to 1950. But the newer units are more complicated, and you will need a good reference manual. At any rate, the mechanic is interested in the internal parts and their condition. In the manual transmission, look for worn bearings, chipped or broken gear teeth, chipped or rounded synchromesh gear teeth, and worn shifting forks.

Because the gears inside the housing must be moved from one position to another, wear is bound to occur in a manual transmission. First to be affected are the synchromesh gears, because their job essentially is to make the changing gears mesh smoothly at all rotational speeds. Next to break will probably be a gear tooth, usually because of harsh treatment, but finally because of metal fatigue. An old transmission, or a new unit that has been shifted many times, may have a worn shifting mechanism. Finally, when worn-away metal mixes with the oil and circulates through the bearings and bushings, these too may fail.

It isn't vital to know exactly how a particular transmission works, or what each gear does. In fact, minor changes are constantly made in manual-gearbox design. The mechanic is more interested in correcting faults. He must carefully inspect each gear, each synchro ring, each part of the shifting apparatus, and then replace worn parts.

As noted above, the synchros are the most common standard-transmission problems. If the car will not remain in second gear upon deceleration, it's a sure bet the synchros are bad. There is no cure for bad synchromesh gears short of new ones! Any other broken gear must also be replaced.

When repairing a transmission, all or a few of the gears and shafts may be removed. Always thoroughly clean the gearbox and parts with solvent, then blow them dry with air. This eliminates metal particles that can do further damage. During reassembly, be careful to get all snap rings in the groove completely, and include an additive, such as STP or Bardahl, in the grease. This will adhere to the metal surfaces and remain for a time, even if the oil disappears.

Transmission seals most often give the amateur mechanic trouble. If the transmission leaks after it is put back together, the seals are improperly installed. Because there are so many different seals and installation methods, the mechanic must follow directions for the specific transmission, and new seals should *always* be used.

Automatic Transmissions

The idea of an automatic transmission is not new. The first true production units were introduced by General Motors back in 1939. However, it was not until the late 1950's that the automatic became good enough to obsolete the manual gearbox.

The basic advantage of an automatic is the absence of a manual clutch between the engine and transmission gears. By utilizing fluid dynamics, a mechanical connection between the driving and driven members can be attained. But this does not mean that all automatic-transmission designs are ideal. They are not. This will not be too important in fixing up an old car if the stock engine is to be used, but whenever an increase in power is contemplated, the early automatic transmission will need help.

In all automatics, a fluid coupling device takes the place of clutch and flywheel. Designs of this coupling are many and varied, but the desired result is the same, to smoothly transmit torque to the gears. As a rule, this coupling will have an outer housing, sealed, that connects to the engine crankshaft flange. Inside this housing will be fluid and attached vanes. Another vaned unit is free to rotate inside the housing, with a shaft leading from the rear of the housing to the transmission. At low rpm, as at idle, the engine rotates the big housing, but the circulation of fluid within the housing is not enough to make the secondary vaned unit turn. However, as the rpm increases, so does the fluid force, until the secondary unit is also turning. A good example of this can be seen when a glass of milk is stirred. As the spoon rotates, the surrounding milk will also begin to rotate. If the rotation is raised to enough rpm, the glass will even begin to rotate.

This basic principle of fluid dynamics is the foundation of all automatics; however, there is much sophistication in its use. For instance, the Chevrolet Power-Glide is not a good heavy-duty automatic to put behind a high-horsepower engine, because of inefficiency in the fluid coupling and weakness in the internal gears and clutches. On the other hand, the four-speed Hydra-Matics produced during the mid-1950's are excellent particularly when reworked with better friction clutches.

The new three-speed automatics (early automatics, such as the PowerGlide, are two-speed) were developed for high-horsepower engines, and all use the Torque Converter fluid coupling. In this type of coupling, a stator is placed in the fluid path, and by ingenious control of the fluid flow, the converter can actually multiply the torque coming from the engine. That is, with a straight clutch or fluid coupling the low gear ratio of 3:1 remains constant. By adding a torque converter, this ratio can be raised to 5:1 or more.

The interior of an automatic transmission can be a bag of snakes to the unwary. A considerable amount of mechanical ingenuity has been packed into a very small space, but hydraulics are still the controlling factor.

The basic transmission function of gears as a torque multiplier remains, but these gears are shifted automatically by the transmission itself, in direct proportion to engine speed. Sliding on the mainshaft of the automatic transmission are clutch assemblies, each assembly in turn connected to a gear set. Engagement of one of these clutch packs also engages the selected gear.

Connected to the mainshaft, usually at the fluid coupling, is an oil pump. As the engine rpm increases, so does the fluid (oil) pressure from this pump. The oil is routed through a special control body, and when a specific pressure is reached, oil directed to a particular clutch pack causes the pack to compress, thereby turning the desired gear. The actual mechanics are complex, but this lay explanation provides a general description of automatic gearbox function.

When an automatic transmission fails, it seldom lets the driver limp home. The car stays where it is. Invariably, an automatic fails in the clutches first, then possibly in the oil pump, and finally in the gears. About the only harsh treatment that will kill an automatic is revving up the engine with the transmission in neutral (which builds up tremendous hydraulic pressures from the oil pump), then slamming the transmission into gear. The sudden explosion of hydraulic pressure on the clutches and gears is murder.

Maintenance and Repair of Automatics

Improper care is the automatic's worst enemy. Failure is almost always traced either to transmission oil that has never been changed or to a low oil level. Transmission oil can and does break down from heat, and, in either case, excessive heat buildup in the clutches induces failure.

As with the manual transmission, repair of an automatic is strictly a matter of remove and replace. The fluid coupling will seldom fail, but if there has been extensive damage inside the transmission case, particles of metal and friction material will fill the coupling. Disassembly of an automatic takes about twice as much time as a standard gearbox, and a reference manual is imperative. If lubrication has been the cause of failure, always suspect bad bearings and perhaps a scored input or mainshaft. Very close tolerances are held in an automatic, so there is no room for sloppiness.

When a transmission repair problem cannot be handled by the amateur, it should be turned over to the professional. But beware; never tear apart a transmission and then ask a professional to reassemble a box load of pieces. The price will be more than the original repair. Individual pieces can be taken to repair shops, however, at a fraction of the overall cost.

Rear Ends

Although often troublesome on older cars, rear ends are not hard to fix. Usually called the final drive, the rear end includes the third member (that portion of the unit which includes the differential gears), the axles, and the axle housing. For the most part, trouble is limited to the first two.

The differential in the final drive is the assembly of gears most directly related to performance. The axle housing, axle shafts, seals, bearings, and retainers serve only to transmit the torque supplied by the engine and modified by the gears in the transmission and differential to the wheels.

The differential has two very basic functions. First, it provides a mounting for gears with ratios that most properly utilize the engine torque to suit specific performance requirements. Second, it properly applies engine torque to the wheels under the variety of conditions encountered in driving.

Automobiles have been equipped with differentials almost since their inception, and most still use a basic mechanical principle developed by a Frenchman named Pecqueor in 1865. The Pecqueor principle involved an ingenious set of gears which could deliver a power input to either one of two output shafts that operated independently of each other. If the load on the output shafts was equal, both would deliver equal torque. If one output shaft was restrained by mechanical resistance, the opposite shaft would deliver the input power.

Early automotive engineers were not long in seizing the Pecqueor principle to solve a basic problem. When one of their first creations turned a corner, the outside rear wheel naturally turned faster than the inside rear wheel. If engine power was applied equally to both rear wheels, the inside wheel could only keep up with the outside wheel by spinning and scuffing its tire against the roadway surface. The Pecqueor principle remains with us today in all cars with the exception of some racing cars.

In conventional differentials, a bevel gear pinion coupled to the driveshaft is meshed with a ring gear bolted to the differential case in the rear-axle housing. The case rotates with the ring gear and carries with it a spider or shaft on which are mounted two or more small bevel pinions that rotate freely on the differential spider or shaft. These smaller bevel pinions are meshed with bevel gears on the ends of the two axle shafts.

If the load on the axle shafts is equal, the small pinions on the spider remain stationary. Then, as the differential case rotates, they function only as a fixed coupling between the case and the axle drive gears. If the load on one of the axle shafts is increased, the bevel gear on the shaft can spin or freewheel the spider gears, and the driving force is delivered to the opposite axle shaft bevel gear.

The conventional differential, utilizing the Pecqueor principle, works fine until one wheel loses traction on a slippery surface. Then all of the engine torque is expended in spinning one wheel while the other does nothing toward propelling the vehicle. In a run-of-the-mill stock car this is not too important unless the driver gets off a dry, hard-surfaced roadway. In a high-performance vehicle, however, this on-again, off-again application of power to the rear wheels can result in reduced efficiency because of the differences in frictional contact which individual driving wheels may have with even dry pavement.

Limited-Slip Differential

The limited-slip differential has a series of small clutch discs within the differential case. These discs have a specific preload and convey torque from the case to the bevel gears on the axle shafts. These clutches allow a certain amount of slip when the rear wheels turn at different speeds. At relatively slow speeds on slippery surfaces, the clutch discs have sufficient friction to keep both axle shafts turning and transmitting equal torque to the driving wheels.

The limited-slip differential has one predominant weakness. The clutches can withstand only a specific preload before they must slip. Excessive slippage between these discs will result in severe wear. If a vehicle is subjected to harsh treatment, it may be expected that the discs will have to be replaced frequently. If the clutch-disc friction is increased by the addition of spacers, the results will be similar to a solid axle with restricted differential action on corners. Noisy opera-

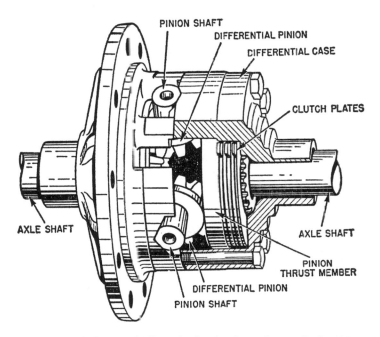

PINION SHAFT
DIFFERENTIAL PINION
DIFFERENTIAL CASE
CLUTCH PLATES
AXLE SHAFT
AXLE SHAFT
PINION
THRUST MEMBER
DIFFERENTIAL PINION
PINION SHAFT

Limited-slip differential allows both wheels to drive vehicle. Wear
occurs inside clutch plate assembly

tion would make use of the car on the street imprac-
tical.

The ratchet, or locking-type, differential does not
use clutches. In this unit the conventional spider gears
are eliminated in favor of a special spider with sprags
that engage matching teeth on clutch driving members.
These driving members transmit torque to the axle-
drive gears. The driving members sandwich a cam gear
that raises the spring-loaded members clear of the

spider drive to allow differential action when the car turns a corner.

Ratchet-type differentials are available in two styles. One uses synchro-type rings to silence the ratcheting noise that occurs on cornering. The other is a standard unit that does not have the synchro feature. This non-synchro type emits a sharp clicking noise as a car negotiates a sharp turn at low speeds.

Repair of Rear Ends

Any repair work on a rear end is usually limited to replacement of worn gears and bearings or broken axles. Occasionally a twisted axle will crop up, but is not a major problem. When trouble strikes a final drive, either the car will not move or excessive noise will come from that area.

If the car will not move, check for a broken axle. Noise indicates wear of the ring or pinion gears, or bad bearings. Always suspect bad bearings first. The axle will have bearings at the hub end and in the carrier housing. All rear ends will have bearings for the pinion shaft. The outboard axle bearings are the normal culprits when a noise is heard, and replacement may or may not require shop facilities. If the bearing is pressed onto the axle end, it can easily be removed and replaced. But if it is stubborn, never use heat. Instead, find a good hydraulic press. In some cases, the bearings are held in place by retainers, and sometimes these retainers must be split with a cold chisel for removal.

When a bearing must be pressed on or off, the best bet is to farm the labor out to a professional.

Work on the pinion gear must be done with the gear removed from the third-member housing. This requires tools that few amateurs own. The pinion shaft is held in the housing at a precise location in relation to the ring gear, and if this relationship is not perfect, excessive wear and noise invariably result.

Pinion shaft bearings and seals can be replaced only by a qualified mechanic, because of the shimming necessary for pinion and ring-gear clearance. The ring gear, however, can be exchanged by anyone as long as the bolt-torque specifications are observed.

To check for worn gears, look closely at the teeth, especially the ring-gear teeth. Put white grease on several of the teeth, and rotate the gears. If the gear mesh is not at the center of the ring-gear tooth, both lengthwise and in depth, something is wrong. Generally, unless an inept mechanic has been working on the rear end, this relationship will be satisfactory. But the teeth can show signs of wear, and should then definitely be replaced.

Axles are either good or bad, and the driver seldom knows which until they fail. However, if a hairline crack is found, or the splines appear to be twisted, the axle should be replaced.

If there is a problem in obtaining replacement gears for a particular third member, it is possible to replace the entire rear end with one from another make of car. This is especially true if you stay within the general line of a manufacturer, such as General Motors or Ford. The major factors here are tread width, wheel-bolt pattern (Pontiac and Olds are identical, as are Ford and Chrysler Imperial), spring mounting, and universal-joint type.

7 Suspension and Brakes

The most important part of any automobile is the suspension and brake system. Usually considered as two distinct systems, they are inextricably woven into a car's total performance, so here they will be treated as one. Unfortunately, too many old cars only get a facelifting, renewed power, and a set of new tires. The old suspension (frame, springs, shocks, axles, etc.) and brakes hardly rate a second glance.

Frames

The early frame designs were simple "ladder" affairs. That is, the two side rails were connected by simple crossmembers. When the all-steel car body came along, frames began to get sophistication. The body helped the frame absorb some of the tremendous torsional forces an automobile sustains. But the first real advance in frame design came when Cord and Auburn introduced the X-member in the late 1920's. This radical design created a much stiffer frame at about the same overall weight.

The early Ford frames provide a prime example of this advance. The 1932 and older Fords (Model A's and T's) utilized the simple ladder—two side rails and three crossmembers. In 1933 this was changed to side rails with front and rear crossmembers and a beefy X-center crossmember. Consequently, the post-1933 Fords have an excellent reputation for frame rigidity.

The condition of an old car frame is almost directly dependent upon basic design and the amount of abuse the frame has received through the years. Naturally, a farm truck is less likely to be perfect than a twenty-year-old Chevrolet long in storage. If the stock engine and suspension are to be fixed up and retained, the original frame can be expected to survive for years. However, any anticipated change in the power (engine hop-up, engine swap, etc.) or suspension (better brakes, bigger rear end, etc.) should be accompanied by careful frame inspection.

Generally, all cars produced after 1928 have basic frames suitable to any kind of use—street, dune buggy, drag racing, and the like—if the center crossmember is made strong enough to carry the heavier engine and transmission combinations. It is advisable to remove the body from the frame during the early stages of fixing up any old car (pre-1949) or at least to remove the four fenders. Inspect the frame rails for fatigue cracks, especially around rivet holes where the cross-members mount. Have these cracks arc welded, and if the rivets have loosened through the years, weld the crossmember directly to the frame.

When modifying a frame for any reason, always be on the safe side. Use at least ¼-inch steel plate for bracing, ³⁄₁₆-inch plate for crossmembers (or minimum 0.090-inch wall tubing), and never trust a nut-and-bolt connection; rivet or weld anything other than simple brackets.

If an engine or transmission is to be swapped, or if the suspension is to be drastically changed, a bodyless frame is far easier to work with. If a sandblasting facility is available, this is the best method for cleaning a frame. Otherwise, rely on elbow grease and a wire brush. Cleaned frames should be lightly coated with Rust-O-Leum, then painted with enamel (lacquer and acrylic chip too easily), using either spray gun or brush.

Frame and suspension advances have been matched during the last two decades by a number of body-construction improvements. Fisher Body led the way with the Turret Top all-steel body in 1934. This body did away with the cloth insert in the top and had steel stampings as part of the body structure in the sides and floor. Unitized construction was introduced about this time also. The body and frame are really made as one piece, with the power train bolting directly to the combination structure.

Late-model Fords have a frame design of Coke-bottle configuration. The frame has a rather narrow bottom-to-top cross-section, boxed for maximum rigidity and strength. Crossmembers are virtually nonexistent. A transmission carrier is located under the front floorboards, and a thin hunk of tubing lies just behind the rear seat. The frame curves toward the outside just behind the front wheels and then narrows just ahead of the rear wheels. For suspension, Ford uses semi-elliptic springs on outboard frame mounts at the rear and coil-sprung A-arms of unequal length at the front. The front has ball-and-joint-carried spindles.

The frame of a Chevrolet, Cadillac, or Buick varies quite a bit from the Ford frame. For both General Motors and Ford, a lowering of body height forced drastic redesign of older frame styles. Ford sets the seats down inside the frame (remember the step-down Hudson?), while the GM approach has been to squeeze the midsection of the frame together, setting the seats down outside the center hump. The result is a rather heavy frame, with the suspension members attached to "add-ons." The front end uses ball-and-joint spindle carriers along with unequal-length A-arms and coil springs. Coils are also used at the rear, with the rear end located by heavy stamped-steel radius rods connecting to outriggers on the "wasp" frame.

Chrysler Corporation uses a combination unit body and frame. The area from the firewall forward is a bolt-on framework that holds the engine and front suspension. Chrysler products all use torsion-bar front springing, which is a definite assist in the handling department. With this type of springing, the lower stamped-steel A-arm serves as the locater for the front

end of the torsion bar. The bar runs rearward along-
side the framework and stops in an adjusting casting.
A heavy bolt may be screwed in or out to adjust spring
tension (and relative height of the front end). Rear
springing of a Chrysler product is by conventional semi-
eliptic springs.

Suspension

The suspension system causes trouble for many an
amateur mechanic. However, as complicated as the
suspension may seem, it is nothing more than a means
of *controlling* the total vehicle mass. Although important, passenger comfort is a secondary consideration.
Because suspension, which includes the steering, is so
vital, the original springs and steering of an old car
should never be changed merely for the sake of change.

Car springs may be divided into three categories:
leaf, coil, and torsion bar. Leaf springs consist of a
stack of long, narrow, and relatively thin strips of
spring steel of unequal length. The individual "leaves"
have an "arch" formed into them, and the spring action
is derived from the arch and the sliding contact between the leaves. The leaf spring reacts to a wide range
of compression and rebound because of the different
degrees of resiliency imparted to the spring by the
various lengths and stiffnesses of the leaves.

The mounting of leaf springs in suspension systems
has taken many forms. These mountings can be de-
scribed as the quarter, semi, three-quarter, and full

elliptic. The full elliptic and three-quarter elliptic springs have long disappeared as automotive components. The full elliptic consisted of two semielliptics pivoted together at the ends of their longest leaves. The upper semielliptic section arched upward toward the frame where it was anchored, and the lower section arched downward, where it was secured to the axle at its center. The three-quarter elliptic consisted of a combination of a semielliptic and a quarter elliptic. The semielliytic was anchored to the frame at one end and had its other end pivoted to a quarter elliptic which was secured to the frame. The quarter elliptics are simply one half of a semielliptic. Quarter elliptics are still used in a few suspension systems but not in conjunction with semielliptics.

Leaf springs are mounted either transversely or longitudinally on the frame. In the case of a transverse mounting, a shackle is necessary at both ends where the spring is secured to the axle. As any leaf spring is compressed, its overall length is increased, and this lateral movement of the spring is given freedom by the shackles. In a transverse system, the springs cannot hold the axles in the necessary perpendicular alignment to the frame, and radius rods are necessary. Radius rods at the front run from the frame to the axle and are pivoted to permit up-and-down movement while canceling out any fore-and-aft movement of the axle. At the rear the function of the radius rods is similar; however, they also serve to transmit the driving force from the rear axle and wheels to the frame.

Semielliptic springs, when used in a longitudinally mounted suspension system, have shackles at their rear anchor points. Front ends of the pairs of springs are secured to the frame and hold the axles in alignment. At the rear, this type of mounting also allows power to be transmitted from the rear axle to the frame through the front halves of the springs.

Coil springs came into prominence in the automotive field with the advent of both front and rear independent wheel-suspension systems. The methods used to incorporate coil springs into a suspension system are varied. However, the basic design elements are similar to those encountered in a transverse leaf-spring system—keeping the wheels in alignment and transmitting power from the rear axle to the frame.

Torsion-bar suspension systems have been used for many years in European automobiles. Packard was one of the first of the U.S. manufacturers to adopt such a system. The Dodge, Plymouth, and Chrysler cars use torsion bars in their current suspension systems. Torsion bars are used extensively in track-racing and competitive sports cars because the characteristics of this type of spring can be easily altered to suit various conditions encountered on a track.

Torsion bars derive their spring action from the inherent resiliency in certain types of steel, which will resist a twisting motion and return to the original shape. A long round spring-steel bar, if secured in a vise at one end and twisted with a pipe wrench at the other end, will tend to resist the pressure applied to the wrench and spring back to its original shape when the pressure is released. This principle is applied to automobiles by anchoring one end of the torsion bar to the frame and the other end to the wheel supports or axles.

Torsion bars are usually made from circular cross-section steel, but this is not necessarily the rule. The Volkswagen, for example, has torsion bars at both the front and rear consisting of rectangular cross-section steel leaves encased in tubes. The mounting of torsion bars in some cases is parallel to the frame, and in others it is transverse or parallel to the axis of the front or rear wheels.

Shock Absorbers

The automotive shock absorber is a spring control device that checks the initial deflection of the spring and then rapidly damps out subsequent spring vibrations. In performing this function, it removes the energy that has been put into the suspension system by road irregularities and dissipates it as heat.

Shock absorbers have come to be commonly known as "shocks," and whether the full nomenclature or its contraction is applied, this description is a misnomer. The British describe the device as a damper, which is a considerably more accurate term. The spring is really the shock-absorbing device, while the function of the shock absorber is to dissipate the energy stored in the spring.

The shock absorber produces its damping action by offering resistance to the movement of the spring when it is displaced from its normal load position. This resistance has the effect of reducing the flexibility of the suspension system and thus transmits some of the shock generated by road irregularities to the chassis. The greater the amount of control exercised by the shock absorbers over the suspension system, the greater these forces become.

A large amount of resistance or control must be provided by the shock absorbers for violent deflections of the springs, such as those which occur on rough roads. However, for average roads, on which relatively small and slow spring deflections occur, only a small amount of control is necessary. The greater the amount of control provided by the shock absorber, the greater the harshness of the ride. Thus the ideal shock absorber is one that will offer only very modest resistance to small and slow spring deflections while providing the high resistance necessary when violent spring deflections are encountered.

Early shock absorbers were of the friction type. The friction shock consisted of two or more metal discs, usually faced with a friction material and held in contact with each other by one or more bolts. Variations in the ride from stiff to soft were obtained by tightening or loosening the bolts that held the discs together. Friction shocks have largely been discarded in favor of the telescoping hydraulic type. However, they are still used on oval-track and drag-racing machines.

The modern telescoping hydraulic shock absorber consists essentially of a piston moving in a hydraulic cylinder and a series of orifices and check valves to control the flow of hydraulic oil above and below the piston. The makes are many and varied in design. Some have an external adjustment to control the flow of hydraulic fluid within the unit and thus increase the amount of control that can be obtained.

Suspension Changes

Modifications in any part of a suspension system must be minimal, unless an authority on the subject has been consulted. Unfortunately, such an authority is very often difficult to locate. Local mechanics seldom are familiar with the technical aspects of the problem, while even the automotive engineer usually lacks knowledge of suspension "swaps." Most often, the amateur mechanic must rely on experienced car enthusiasts.

A suspension system should never be modified to conform with a fad. For instance, the practice of raising the frame of a car—increasing the distance between the frame/body and suspension/wheels—should never be followed in a road car. This change raises the bulk mass of a vehicle and is strictly a function of serious quarter-mile drag racing. It is made to increase the fore-aft weight transfer potential. Obviously, the side-to-side weight transfer will also be affected, and cornering or stopping will be hazardous.

As a guide to suspension changes, the old car with a beam front axle using two semielliptic springs (GM and Chrysler products) should have the springs tailored to the final car weight. That is, if the stock engine is retained, the springs may be disassembled and cleaned, then reinstalled. A transverse spring (pre-1949 Fords) should be treated likewise. However, if a heavier engine is used, the springs may need an addition of one to three leaves. These leaves should be almost as long as the main leaf in order to maintain a reasonably soft ride. Short spring leaves give a stiffer ride. Rear leaf springs are treated in the same way.

A car using independent front suspension and coil springs is much harder to work with than one with leaf springs. Accordingly, only the experienced professional should attempt any radical front-end modifications on this type of suspension. Because a coil spring is nothing more than a wound torsion bar, it will tend to sag with age. Also, these coil springs are designed for the specific weight of the car. If the engine and transmission combination is changed, the springs must also be changed. Generally speaking, an engine swap into a 1955 or earlier car will require stronger front springs.

The spring rate (strength) is directly related to overall coil diameter, wire diameter, and height. In a specific application, the coil diameter and height are already determined, so only the wire size can change. On cars made after 1948, station-wagon springs of the same-make car will usually do the trick and offset an additional 100 to 300 pounds on the front end.

A spring of any type should never be heated and re-shaped except by a spring shop. Spring material is specially created and must be worked carefully; otherwise the "temper" is removed and the spring becomes just another piece of steel.

Steering

Steering is one area where some experimentation can be attempted with relative safety. Every year the engineers make better and better steering units; therefore, the steering gearbox from a twenty-five-year-old car can be replaced by a newer one that is considerably better.

The original steering can often be rebuilt with parts available through most auto-parts stores or car agencies. However, these old units will still be of obsolete design. When selecting a late-model steering gear, always use the same basic type as the original. If a drag-link design is stock (drag link parallel to the frame), similar designs are available for Ford, Chevrolet, and GMC pickups utilizing beam and axles. If a cross-link is used (the drag link is transverse, or a part of the tie-rod function), almost any new car uses a similar system. The major caution in steering modification is always to have any steering-shaft or link welding done by a professional, and make sure the gearbox is mounted solidly to the frame.

Brakes

Brakes are an especially critical part of any mobile vehicle. Although an anchor and a long rope may work for the sailing ship, such an arrangement is hardly practical for automobiles. When the wheel first became a part of man's environment, it allowed a tremendous stride forward in transportation. And as wheel transportation progressed, the need for a better brake cropped up. At first, the old wagon relied on a leather-covered wooden pad pressed against the wheel rim. But the faster the speed or the greater the load, the more ineffectual this type of design proved. The early horseless carriages made before 1900 found the drum-type brake essential.

These early drum brakes consisted of a flexible metal band, lined with woven asbestos material, and a drum, around which the band was wrapped. The next step forward came with the development of the internal expanding shoe brake. In these brakes, a pair of shoes faced with frictional material were suspended within the brake drum. The shoes were pivoted at one end and had a cam located between their free ends. When the brakes were applied, the cams rotated, through a system of levers, to force the shoes against the drum.

The earliest automobiles had brakes only on the rear wheels, and this was considered adequate for the conditions of the day. As the power and speed of automobiles increased, however, the need for brakes that could supply more stopping power became increasingly evident. As a result, designers began to investigate the possibility of doubling brake effectiveness by placing brakes on the front wheels, also.

Unfortunately, brakes on the front wheels involved some knotty problems that required years to solve. Adjusting and equalizing a leverage system so equal pressure could be applied to all brake shoes or bands was only one of these problems. Brakes on the front wheels, because of the erratic and unpredictable action of the system, made them more of a hazard than a help.

Despite problems, the first four-wheel brakes made an appearance on the British Phoenix racing cars in 1908 and were shortly followed by the Italian Isotta-Fraschini in 1910 and the Scottish Argyle in 1911. Still, braking systems were far from ideal, and four-wheel systems remained relatively unpopular for another decade.

The Argyle cars used one of the mechanical brake designs derived from the genius of a Frenchman named Henri Perrot. After World War I, an American, Vincent Bendix, acquired the patents to the Perrot system for use in the United States. This subsequently led to the development of the famous Bendix brake. By 1923 the first mechanically operated four-wheel brake systems were announced as components of American stock cars.

While manufacturers were tinkering with the tricky mechanical four-wheel systems, Malcolm Lockheed, a Californian, was busy seeking a substitute for mechanical brake linkage. His efforts first appeared on the 1921 Duesenberg racing cars in the form of four-wheel, hy-

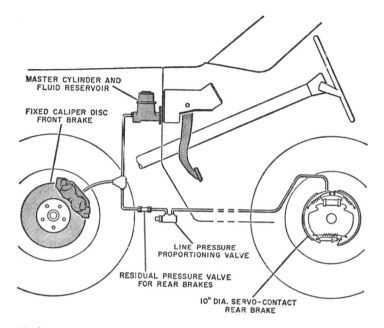

MASTER CYLINDER AND
FLUID RESERVOIR

FIXED CALIPER DISC
FRONT BRAKE

LINE PRESSURE
PROPORTIONING VALVE

RESIDUAL PRESSURE VALVE
FOR REAR BRAKES

10" DIA. SERVO-CONTACT
REAR BRAKE

Modern combination of drum rear brakes and disc front brakes
will be standard practice on most cars by the end of the 1960's.

draulically operated, external-contracting band brakes.
The success of Lockheed was based on the principle
that any pressure exerted at any point on a confined
fluid will transmit this pressure through the fluid
equally in all directions. It thus became possible to
transmit brake pedal pressure equally to the brakes on
all four wheels. By 1939, all major American car builders had adopted the hydraulic system.

Practically all brakes in use today are either the drum
type with internal expanding shoes or the disc type

(discussed later), and they are called upon to do a tremendous job. Brakes fulfill their purpose by converting mechanical energy to heat, which is generated by the frictional contact between the shoe facings and the drum, or the pads and disc in a disc-type brake. The heat, in turn, must be dissipated by the drum or disc.

If 100 horsepower will accelerate a 3500-pound vehicle to 60 miles per hour in 750 feet and the brakes are required to stop it in 150 feet, the brakes must dissipate five times the torque exerted by the engine, or the equivalent of 500 horsepower. It has been estimated that the heat developed by brakes during a normal day's driving would heat a small house during winter weather for 24 hours. One hard, crash stop from 75 miles per hour in some cars can induce complete "fade"—that is, the drum becomes so hot that it expands away from the shoe and renders the brakes completely ineffective until the brakes are given a 15- or 20-minute cooling period. Heat dissipation has been and continues to be a big factor in brake design.

In an automotive brake system, the shoes that face toward the front of the car are called the primary or leading shoes. The units that face to the rear are referred to as secondary or trailing. When the car moves forward and the brakes are applied, the friction on the leading shoe attained by brake pedal pressure is increased, since the shoe leans into the drum. This is called the self-energizing effect. The opposite happens to the trailing shoe, which pushes away from the drum. When braking in reverse, the secondard shoe becomes the self-energizing shoe, and vice versa. This system has been used on several cars, including Fords, Mercurys, and some models of Lincoln from 1939 through 1948. The system is simple and dependable.

This self-energizing effect brings up an interesting point—that the effectiveness of the self-energizing shoe is usually about twice that of the trailing shoe. Consequently, the lining on the leading shoes is shorter than that on the secondary shoe, and thicker. The front shoe is doing more work and will wear faster. The problem here is to equalize as much as possible the braking forces between the two shoes, thus the difference in shoe lining. In addition, the wheel hydraulic cylinders are usually step-bored, with the piston actuating the secondary slightly larger than that moving the leading shoe. The disadvantage of such a system is extra loading of the wheel bearings when the brakes are used. This loading is directly proportional to the braking force differential between the primary and secondary shoes, the diameter of the brake drum, and the location of the brake assembly in relation to the bearings.

Rather common on foreign cars and used for some years in the United States by the Chrysler Corporation is the system with two leading shoes. This layout takes full advantage of the self-energizing effect in that each shoe is a primary or leading shoe connected at its toe to its own cylinder. The cylinders are located 180 degrees from each other at the top and bottom of the backing plate. The front shoe is operated by the top cylinder; the bottom cylinder operates the back shoe. Each shoe then benefits from the self-energizing effect, since it faces the direction of drum rotation. Linings on both shoes are identical. The two cylinders are joined by a common hydraulic line that equalizes cylinder pressure. The heel of each shoe is pivotally anchored, but instead of being close together as before, the anchors are diametrically opposed. Adjustments are through eccentrics or ratchets. This arrangement is usually found only on the front brakes in American cars.

The twin-leading-shoe brakes take maximum advantage of the self-energizing effect. They require less pedal pressure and produce less strain on the front wheel bearings. But then, a disadvantage is quick heat buildup under extreme or prolonged use, which may result in fade. The tendency to lock or grab is greater if water, dirt, etc., happen to get between the shoe and the drum, but this isn't a major problem. Designs with three and four leading shoes have been tried but are not common.

It has been mentioned that modern brake systems are dependent on the basic hydraulic principle that any pressure exerted on a fluid is transmitted equally in all directions. Hydraulic brake systems use a specially compounded oil that will not deteriorate the various rubber-compounded seals and lines in the system. In addition, these hydraulic fluids are relatively incompressible at the pressures and temperatures that crop up in an automobile braking system.

In a closed hydraulic system of any sort, if one cubic

inch of fluid in the master cylinder is pushed on by the brake pedal, a like amount of fluid must be displaced in the rest of the hydraulic system. In the automobile system, the clearance between brake shoes at rest and the drum provide the area for the fluid to be displaced to, in a manner of speaking. Of course, it takes a really tremendous amount of pressure at each brake shoe to stop a two-ton hulk of automobile, an amount of pressure that certainly no human could provide if he pushed directly on the master cylinder piston. Therefore, the laws of leverage are placed into effect at the brake pedal.

The brake pedal is basically a pendulum affair, with a foot pad at one end. The other end of the pedal arm is secured to some portion of the body or frame structure, with the arm free to swing fore and aft only. Slightly below this connection (or above, as the case may be) the pedal arm is connected to the master cylinder via a piston rod. Through the leverage provided by this arrangement, a few pounds of force at the pedal produce much more pressure at the master cylinder and several thousand pounds of pressure at the wheel cylinders.

For example, suppose the brake-pedal arm is 10 inches long from the foot pad to the pivot point. If the distance from the center of the pivot point to the center of the bolt attaching the master cylinder rod and pedal arm together is 1 inch, the lever advantage is a strong 10 to 1. So 65 pounds of force on the brake pedal will result in 650 pounds at the master-cylinder piston.

Now, if the master-cylinder bore is just 1 inch, the hydraulic line pressure will be the area of the master-cylinder piston (0.7854 square inches) multiplied by the force applied to the piston, or 510.5 pounds per square inch.

On cars produced since 1950, the line pressure may vary from 650 pounds per square inch up (65 pounds initial force), with power-brake boosters giving figures often three times greater. The combined mechanical leverage and hydraulic advantage thus form a ratio of roughly 80 to 1 between the pedal and the brake shoes. So, if the driver pushes on the brake pedal to the tune of 65 pounds, the radial pressure of the shoes on the drums is 5200 pounds. This example does not take into account that the actual efficiency of such a mechanical and hydraulic linkage is closer to 90 percent than 100. On the other hand, it must be remembered that most braking systems use at least one leading shoe, and the self-energizing effect just about doubles the effect of a nonenergized shoe.

From the foregoing, it is easy to see that the enterprising mechanic can come up with an infinite number of brake actions and ratios merely by varying the leverage between the pedal and master cylinder or between the master cylinder and wheel-cylinder piston area. Then too, the substance used on the brake lining as a friction surface and the method in which the shoes are applied may also be altered at will with a little thought and junkyard searching.

Through the use of step-bored wheel cylinders and

a constant pedal pressure (65 pounds being considered about maximum for a panic-stop situation), we could either put more pressure on the trailing or nonenergized shoe to equalize shoe pressure, or more pressure on the leading shoe to take more advantage of the self-energizing effect and get lighter pedal pressure. The average American car has a front and rear braking effectiveness of about 65 and 35 percent, respectively. A very light (2000-pound) early car might have more weight on the rear wheels, and thus the above ratio might prove too much on the front, not enough on the rear. A 60–40 ratio is about right for a front-engine car, 55–45 for a rear engine.

Among many special car builders it is felt that the braking ratio between the front and rear wheels should be such that the front wheels are still a bit short of skidding when the rear wheels are on the point of skidding. This ratio depends on the leverage of the brakes, shoe design, anchorage, shoe-lining friction, weight distribution, and weight transfer during braking.

If the 2000-pound car has about 50–50 weight distribution—for example, most early Fords fitted with Chevy V8 engines—and 1940 or later Ford brakes have been fitted, more braking effectiveness may have to be built into the rear systems. This could be in the form of step-bored wheel cylinders to give the leading shoes more of the self-energizing effect. It must be pointed out here that by arbitrarily bolting various car parts together one cannot hope to always achieve the best in braking. An amateur mechanic who builds a car in this manner may never experience any real difficulty, but then neither does he tax the braking system to its maximum efficiency.

One example of this problem is the use of late-model rear ends in something like a Model A coupe. Usually, the front brakes are taken from a 1940 Ford or similar car. They are of the aforementioned single-leading-shoe type. The rear end is from a Chevy or Oldsmobile of the 1950's, and no thought is given to braking ratios. All of a sudden the driver may find the rear wheels locking for no apparent reason. There is a reason, of course. The late-model rear end has brakes designed for a 4000-pound car. The car weighs about 2000 pounds. Also, the front brakes were designed for a car weighing about 3000 pounds. One of two courses of action is indicated: either make the wheel cylinders in the rear brakes smaller or transfer to Bendix brakes for the front. Utilizing the Bendix units seems to be the best, since they were used on some Lincoln cars up to 1948 and will bolt right onto the other Ford-product spindles. Remember that this is still only an approximation of the real thing, and a little figuring of weight distribution and ratios is necessary to get the top job.

If you have a mechanical system and for some reason or other cannot change to hydraulics, all is not lost. You can do the same kind of adjusting and experimenting with mechanical brakes and come up with reasonable results. Just be prepared to keep a constant check on the system and know that adjustment is almost always necessary. In the mechanical system, a cam takes the place of the wheel cylinder, and by playing around with operating-arm lengths you can get a variety of pedal and shoe pressures.

One of the greatest advantages to the hydraulic brake system is that in a fluid system any pressure variation anywhere in the entire system is instantaneous and exactly equal everywhere. If one brake shoe happens to be closer to a drum than all the rest, it will touch the drum first when the brakes are used. But, it won't really do anything drastic until all the other shoes in the system reach the same point of pressure. It is easy to see, then, that this one property of fluids makes extremely close adjustments in a hydraulic system unnecessary. Another advantage is that there is no lost motion in a hydraulic system, and routing of the hydraulic lines is relatively simple. Lines should be clamped every two feet or so, preferably well inside the frame structure out of the way of possible flying rocks and the like.

Maintenance and Repair

If you have had any experience at all with brake systems, you have heard it said time and again that the two greatest enemies of the master cylinder (and, in effect, the entire system) are water and dirt. And for a good reason. Since the reservoir is vented to the open air, condensation water can form on the walls above the fluid level when temperature and humidity vacillate.

The specific gravity of water is greater than that of brake fluid, so it naturally seeps to the bottom of the reservoir and eventually through the ports into the bore. Since the fluid and the water both have an oxygen content, the cast-iron cylinder bore is susceptible to corrosion and eventual scoring of the primary cup. As for dirt, this can be avoided by really cleaning the area around the reservoir filler cap before inspection, and then carefully removing and replacing the cap. Wear of the master cylinder bore due to either of these conditions will usually result in a need for increased pedal pressure; a necessity to pump the pedal; or, with prolonged pedal pressure, a pedal that slowly creeps to the floor. The same symptoms can indicate a leak somewhere in the lines or wheel cylinders, but normally the master cylinder will show signs of wear first.

The rigid lines of a car's brake system are seamed steel tubing with an inside diameter of $\frac{1}{8}$ to $\frac{3}{16}$ inch. Never, never use copper for brake lines. It will crack under certain conditions and will tend to swell more than steel under the high pressures in a hydraulic system. On the other hand, just because tubing looks like copper doesn't mean it is. Some brake-line tubing is coated with copper; to be certain, check a freshly cut end. The steel color will be unmistakable. Lines should be free of kinks and flattened spots that might restrict flow. Forget the outdated slip-on ferrule-type end fittings unless you are absolutely forced to use them. Flared connections are much the best, and a double flaring tool costs very little at the corner hardware store.

At the fore and aft ends of the brake lines, flexible hoses connect to the wheel cylinders. Two hoses will be used at the front and usually just one hose at the rear. As for hose, be sure and buy a good brand and install it in such a manner that it doesn't get sawed off by flailing shocks, steering apparatus, or springs.

Repair of any brake system, hydraulic or mechanical, will usually center around parts replacement. The brake drums must be turned down by a professional mechanic to get rid of any ridges on the drum surface. The brake shoes selected should always be of the best quality, preferably bonded. When overhauling a hydraulic system, the master and wheel cylinders may be repaired by honing the cylinders and installing new pistons and seals, but it is usually cheaper to buy new replacement parts.

After the brake job is finished, put the best quality heavy-duty hydraulic fluid in the system, and bleed the lines. Bleeding is done by starting at the wheel farthest from the master cylinder and working forward. Have someone pump on the brake pedal, then hold it firm while you open the bleed bolt located on the wheel cylinder. Trapped air will spew from this fitting, and when a steady stream of fluid appears, shut the bleed valve. If the brake pedal still feels mushy after bleeding, or suddenly you don't have brakes, air is still trapped in the line.

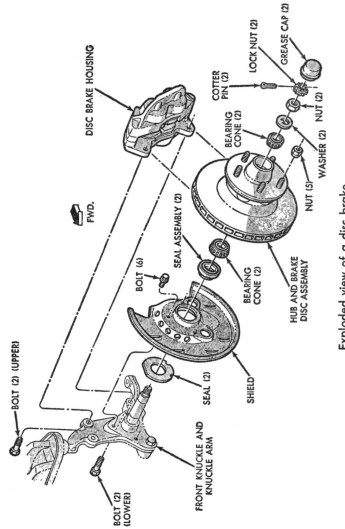

BOLT (2) (UPPER)

DISC BRAKE HOUSING

COTTER PIN (2)

LOCK NUT (2)

GREASE CAP (2)

FWD.

BEARING CONE (2)

NUT (2)

WASHER (2)

SEAL ASSEMBLY (2)

BOLT (6)

BEARING CONE (2)

NUT (5)

HUB AND BRAKE DISC ASSEMBLY

SEAL (2)

SHIELD

FRONT KNUCKLE AND KNUCKLE ARM

BOLT (2) (LOWER)

Exploded view of a disc brake.

Disc Brakes

Disc brakes consist of a flat disc at each wheel and one or more pairs of friction-biscuit "pads" or "pucks" which squeeze tightly against the disc when the brakes are applied. The chief advantage of a disc brake is its ability to resist fade. This characteristic is due, in large measure, to the open design, which allows the air flow around the disc and biscuits to carry away the tremendous heat generated by the braking action.

Another advantage of the disc brake is a greatly increased friction area compared to similar-size drum units. In some cases the disc units may even prove to be lighter than their drum counterparts. The dimensional stability of disc brakes is also very high and remains relatively unaffected by widely varying temperature conditions. One of the disadvantages of disc brakes is that slack wheel bearings allow the disc to move axially, tending to push the pads away from the discs.

Disc brakes are not common on U.S. cars produced before 1965, and very few Detroit disc-brake units will simply bolt up to older cars. Therefore, putting disc brakes on an older car is usually a matter of modifying foreign systems to fit or buying special kits through speed-equipment shops.

8 Wiring

There is absolutely nothing so frustrating to an amateur mechanic as the complexity of wires, gages, relays, and related parts normally associated with the automotive electrical system. At first glance, the entire scheme seems an evil plot designed to destroy mankind; for the novice charging blindly ahead without planning, it is seldom anything else. Although the basics of automotive electricity seem simple enough in themselves, the sheer number of specialized components, particularly on newer cars, tends to drive the average weekend tinkerer away.

Anyone who has ever worked on cars has faced the dilemma of what to do about the wiring, whether the project has been a $15 Model T or a $15,000 Indianapolis racer. The problem can arise with the mere addition of an extra gage, an engine swap, or the complete rebuilding of a highway veteran. Although the complexity will vary, the approach is always the same and may be applied to whatever automotive project is at hand.

Of course, it is wise to have at least a rudimentary grasp of the whys and wherefores of the workings of electricity before going too far. A word always heard when electricity is discussed is *voltage*. This is nothing more than a measure of pressure, much the same as inches are a measure of length. Another electrical term is *amps* (amperes), a measurement of current flow through the wire circuit. Last of all is resistance to current flow, measured in *ohms*.

For simplicity of explanation, let's use the analogy of water and water pipe to electricity and wire.

The amperes, or current flow, can be compared to the flow of water in a pipe. The water cannot move unless it is pushed; this can be accomplished by a pump or some kind of physical pressure. The electrons in the wire cannot move unless they are pushed; this is accomplished by a generator or battery. The voltage is the pressure exerted upon the electrons in the wire. When water is being pumped through a pipe, just so much water will come out of the several taps. If we want more water from one of the taps, we either raise the water pressure or close some of the taps. The resistance to current flow may be likened to the restriction of water flow determined by the size of the water pipe.

If we have wire of a certain size and too many things are powered from it, they will not receive all the current they need to function properly. The wire must be large enough to carry all the current to supply all of the items in the particular circuit. For example, suppose we have a 3-amp radio, a 2-amp windshield-wiper motor, and lighting that requires 7 amps. If these are all connected to a wire rated at 7 amps, it is obvious that they cannot be supplied with the total 12 amps required when everything is turned on at once. The wire would heat up and possibly burn. So use care when selecting wire.

The following handy table can be used for reference to determine the proper size of wire for general automotive use.

Wire Size	Amperage for Safe Use
8–9	35 a
10–11	25 a
12–13	20 a
14–15	15 a
16–17	7 a
18–19	5 a
20–22	3 a

	Wire Size	
Use	12 v	6 v
Headlights	16	12
Taillights	16	12
Turn Signals	16	12
Radio	16	12
Heater	16	12
Parking lights	16	12
Ignition	16	12
Starter	10	8
Ammeter	10	8
Gages	16	12

Use	Wire Size	
	12 v	*6 v*
Fuel pump	16	12
Generator armature	10	8
Generator field	16	12
Generator	16	12

Wire larger than necessary may always be used, but never use wire smaller than that demanded by the particular installation.

It is always easiest to work with the stock wiring harness if possible. Even when an older car normally equipped with a 6-volt electrical system is converted to 12 volts, the original wires are still quite usable.

Never overlook the possibility of buying a new wiring harness (sometimes called wiring loom) from a car dealer or auto-parts store. Suppose you have a 1939 Plymouth sedan with very poor wiring. Check first with local Chrysler Corporation dealers in the area. If a dealership has been established for many years, the item you want may be gathering dust in the attic. Also, check with the local parts houses, and don't overlook the wrecking yard. The old junker may still have decent wiring. Next, look through the Sears and Montgomery Ward catalogues. These two mail-order companies do a tremendous volume of auto-parts business, including the sale of wiring harness. Finally, contact the obsolete-car-parts stores (addresses are contained in the Appendix). It is always a pleasant surprise to find just the equipment needed.

If special work has been done, such as switching engines, the stock wiring harness is still usable. About all an engine swap requires of the electrical system is possible extension of the existing wires to ignition coil, generator, alternator, and temperature and oil-pressure sending units. If a change to the 12-volt system is dictated, merely install a 12-volt battery and place a voltage restrictor (cut-down) in the system. Such restrictors are available through all auto-parts houses as well as Sears or Montgomery Ward. If you want to switch to 12 volts throughout the system, the instruments must be changed, or protected by a restrictor, and all light bulbs must be changed.

If the original wiring harness is like most of those on older cars, some of the wiring will be excellent, some will be bad. The bad portions are usually exposed to the weather, under the body or hood. It is a simple matter to replace this wiring or even make spot repairs, but always use wire of the proper size, splice with the right kind of connection, and protect the new wiring.

The novice mechanic seldom attempts a complete wiring job from scratch, although it is not a difficult project. Yet even for the simplest of jobs there must be a starting point. A carpenter uses a blueprint, a traveler has a map, and the enthusiast wiring his car should have a good outline or plan to follow.

At first glance a wiring diagram may seem rather complex, or even overwhelmingly confusing. But look again, and pay particular attention to the make-up of the plan. The diagram is nothing more than a picture of the wiring, the related parts, and their positions in the car.

In order to have a good start, first make a complete list of all gages, switches, and components in the car that need to be wired. With this list as the initial guide, draw the various parts on paper about where they are to appear on the car. This simple but generally overlooked initial step in wiring will be of great assistance in the layout of the wiring harnesses and cables. The procedure also gives the mechanic a reasonable insight into the amount of wire and number of parts needed for the job.

About now the mechanic should do some future planning on troubleshooting. If you have ever had to trace a wire from the dashboard switch to the taillight when there were several of the same color going in the same direction, you know that this can be frustrating. Here's where wire color-coding comes in. In 16-gage wire at least eighteen different colors are available commercially, and in 12-gage at least eight colors are available. Try to standardize wire colors. For example, all ground wires are usually black, red wires are usually hot battery leads, blue might be for water temperature, brown for oil pressure, etc. Colors are available in enough sizes to allow most wiring in a car to be coded. When selecting colors and wire sizes, note them on the wiring diagram for future reference.

After the wires have been selected, determine how they are to be routed and the kind of protection they will require. When laying out the wires for a harness, there are several things to consider. One is the number of harnesses and cables required; the fewer used, the neater the job. Installation of the wiring systems in a car are generally of two types, semipermanent and quick-disconnect. An example of the semipermanent type is the wiring system on a standard automobile. You can get the harness off the car if you work at it, but it takes time. Much simpler is the quick-disconnect method, which is fast finding favor with special-car builders. These harnesses have common aircraft plug-in disconnects (easily obtainable at electronics parts houses and surplus outlets).

One popular arrangement is to use a single harness from the engine to the firewall with a quick-disconnect (so the engine can be removed without disturbing any wiring), another harness for lights and accessories at the rear of the car, and still another for lights and accessories at the front of the car. All harnesses should have quick-disconnect plugs for easy servicing and removal. The plugs usually line up adjacent to each other near the firewall. The other halves of the plugs have applicable leads from terminal blocks, gages, and switches. When harnesses are properly constructed, no wire should have to be cut or unsoldered to remove any electrical equipment from the car.

When routing the harness through the car, keep all wiring together and near the items being wired. A compact job will be much easier to service in the future. Take extra care to keep the harnesses away from the exhaust and rough or sharp metal edges that might wear through the insulation and cause a short, fire, etc. If a harness or individual wires are exposed to such a danger, enclose them in plastic tubing or some similar substance and then check this area periodically.

Battery cables also need protection. If the battery is in the trunk, cables should be routed along the frame so they do not hang below the frame bottom or pass through any area where they could be pinched. One of the most common errors found on an old car with starting problems is the lack of a good ground. If the battery is too far from the engine for a direct ground cable, make sure that both the battery and the engine ground to the frame.

When clamping cables or harnesses, make neat corners and do not span excessive open spaces. Be very careful of places between body, frame, and suspension where wiring could be pinched. Older chassis and bodies "work" quite a bit during normal use, and a stray wire can easily be rubbed or pinched.

A word about the engine harness. Try to keep this harness completely on one side of the engine if possible. The less wiring on the engine proper, the less trouble that can arise in the future. Generally speaking, the engine harness will contain the water-temperature, oil-pressure, generator, and ignition wires. Wiring and harness material used around the engine should be selected with heat resistance in mind.

Wiring that runs to the lights and accessories at the front and rear of the car is prone to damage if it is not protected. "Spaghetti" (a form of plastic tubing used extensively in aircraft wiring), conduit pipe, lacing, and frame enclosure are all forms of protection. Special lacing on a show car is pretty; plastic spaghetti on a street machine is simple and practical; steel tubing on a dune buggy or mountain goat is ideal for maximum protection.

Let's take plastic tubing first. When the wires have been cut to the proper length and are ready for the tubing, make sure the tubing size is large enough to handle the bundle. As an aid in getting the bundle of wires through the tubing, strip the ends of the wires and solder them neatly together. Then run a piece of steel wire through the tubing, twist one end around the bundle of wires, and tape the union so there won't be any jagged edges. Talcum powder or a similar substance sprinkled inside the tubing and on the bundle of wires will help the insertion procedure. Pulling on the steel wire will lead the wiring bundle into the tubing.

Lacing—used on special show and race cars, and on some antiques—gives a finely detail wiring harness that is hard to beat for appearance. Such work is often seen in special aircraft and missiles, but it is slow and painstaking. The first thing to remember about lacing is that a fine job is only as good as the layout of the wires in the bundle. Straighten each wire in the bundle until you can follow the individual strands from one end of the bundle to the other.

From a roll of lacing twine (available through any local electronics wholesale outlet), reel out a piece three to four times as long as the bundle being laced. Start at one end, preferably the one having the most leads. Tie the end of the bundle as tightly as possible, using two turns around the bundle and a square knot. This is the beginning of the lacing and absolutely must not slip! Now pass the twine under the bundle from left to right, pass back over the beginning lead, tuck under in the direction of travel, and pull through the loop. This gives a simple overhand knot. As the lacing is pulled taut, the piece being pulled must come out under the loop. Repeat this procedure the length of the harness, with the loops half an inch apart. When a breakout is reached (a place where one wire leaves the bundle), use two loops on each side of the breakout, one tied on top of the other. Stop the lacing at the last breakout where only two wires are left. Tie a double loop and a very tight square knot, trim off the excess, and you're through.

It is essential that the initial knot and the ensuing loops be tied correctly and pulled very tight; otherwise the loops will slide on the bundle.

When installing harnesses, individual wires, or cables throughout the car, don't spare the clamps and brackets. Try to clamp wiring securely every 10 inches or so. Use a minimum $\frac{5}{32}$ bolt and nut if possible.

Soldering is an important phase of wiring, no matter how minute the project. Following are some hints so you can do a better job. First of all, use a good iron of approximately 100 to 150 watts. Select a good rosin-core 50–50 solder; do not use acid-core solder, as it will tend to eat up the wire over a period of time. During the job, keep the iron as clean as possible by frequently wiping it on a damp, folded rag. A note of caution: solder will ensure a good electrical connection but should not be used to take mechanical strain.

Strip the ends of the wire, and knot, twist, or in some manner secure the wires to be soldered. Bring the soldering-iron temperature up to working range—hot enough to melt the solder readily. Lay the solder directly on the proposed joint and lay the iron on top of the solder. When the solder flows, remove the iron, taking care not to move the joint during soldering or cooling.

In many instances it will be necessary to splice wires together—for example, at the lights or the electric fuel pump. There are several splice choices. First is to strip the wire, solder, and tape. Second is to strip the wire and install pin ends that push into a common plug. Third is the solderless crimp splice. Bare wire ends are inserted into an insulated splicer, and the splicer is then crimped with a special tool available at most parts houses. When a splice is made where the wires will need to be separated, such as at headlights, the pin and plug may be best; otherwise the last method is most popular.

Invariably, the ends of the wires need some kind of attaching device or tip (commonly called a lug). There are kinds and sizes available to suit any job. You can choose either the kind of lug that slips under a screw or bolt head or the full-circle type, and attach it with either solder or a crimp.

If a quick-disconnect plug is to be used, slip the dust cover over the wire harness. If some small tubing is available, cut short lengths and insert over the end of each wire after the individual wire ends have been stripped about a quarter-inch back. Solder each wire to a pin on the plug. If you don't have the small plastic tubing for insulation, tape each bare area before it has a chance to cool to insure a good seal. Now slip the dust cover onto the plug. When preparing the other half of the plug, make sure that all wires connect to corresponding pins. Make note of the pin numbers on the plug for future reference.

When placing wiring in a tight spot such as behind a dash, the terminal block is a most useful item. It has the ability to give good, clean, multiple connections. For example, powering ten pieces of equipment could require ten battery leads from the ignition switch or jumper leads between each unit. It's much simpler to use a terminal block; bring one hot lead to it and then use short jumpers to the rest of the terminals on the block. All the powered items can now get electricity from the block, and you will still have a neat harness.

Close by the terminal block is the appropriate place for fuses. They are not entirely necessary if the car is insured against fire but they are handy for troubleshooting and as a safety switch. A fuse for the entire wiring system isn't feasible; neither is a single fuse for each wire. It is best to run several wires through one fuse, several through another, and so on. Each group should be fused as close to the current requirement as possible. Too high a rating on a particular fuse could result in the wire heating and burning before the fuse blows.

Up to this point we've discussed all the types of wiring on a car but one—the ignition lead. In most cases this wire is exactly the same as all the others, except for the insulation. Most ignition wire sold today will do a good job on a stock engine, but as the wire gets old it will have suffered from extreme heat and cold, grease, oil, and constant vibration. After such wear and tear it is still handling 10,000 to 20,000 volts! With all this aging and abuse, the insulation starts to break down. The engine will begin to run erratically and miss, gas mileage gets bad, etc. Lift the hood of an older car at night with the lights out, rev the engine, and chances are you will see little flashes of blue all around the ignition wires. If they don't arc to the nearest metal, they will arc to each other.

Several kinds and brands of wire presently on the market will carry the higher voltages and even resist heat, oil, grease, and average wear much better than the common secondary wire. Of course, the price is higher. Packard 440 has long been a favorite among mechanics, and the new Packard 535 and 536 wire promises good things. The 535 has silicone-compound insulation with copper wire, while 536 has the same insulation with stainless-steel wire. Another new secondary wire that is finding favor is Autolite 7 SH, which is showing up everywhere. The orange-colored Autolite wire also has a stainless-steel conductor with a silicone-compound insulation for high heat resistance. It won't burn if it brushes against an exhaust manifold, but it's expensive. Wiry Joe, a long-standing name in automotive wire, also has a good secondary wire on the market. Called Vu-Tron 8, it, too, is being used more and more in specialty installations. With these kinds of special ignition wire, corona losses (voltage losses through the insulation into the air) are almost zero. Leakage is also virtually zero. Nearly all brands of secondary wire on the market may be obtained in ready-made kit form or bought from a roll.

As a review:

1. Construct a good wiring diagram.
2. Choose wire sizes and colors with care.
3. Lay out and route the harness carefully.
4. Select the best harness covering for each application.
5. Select the most appropriate terminal blocks and connecting plugs available.
6. Use care on all labor for the best possible job.

Now, all you have to do is convert several hundred feet of wire into a working wiring system. It's a lot easier than you think; all you have to do is start!

9 The Body and Paint Story

To anyone fixing up a car, the nut-and-bolt procedures are considered within the realm of the most unskilled. But body work or painting is something else again. It seems to be a magic trade practiced by skilled artisans, a form of metal sculpturing totally alien to average person. Don't you believe it! As with anything else conceived by the human mind, mastery is a matter of planning and practice. The big difference between an amateur and a professional body man or painter is time. One is slow, the other fast.

Don't be afraid to tackle any body repair or paint problem, but do so realizing that a single blunder can mean hours of rework. More than any other aspect of do-it-yourself automotive repair, metalwork and painting are processes that should be carefully observed by the beginner before he attempts either. Most body men and painters are proud of their hard-won skills and are more than willing to show a novice the secrets.

Several basic tools are required. A gas welding outfit is essential for major jobs, and the painting equipment must be of the finest. Both may be rented or borrowed. However, some small hand tools are best purchased. You will need a pick hammer; two dollies, one flat and one railroad; a body file for metal and fiberglass; and an inexpensive pop-rivet gun. Total price for this equipment, which may be used many times through the years, will come to less than $25.

Body Work

The amount of body work required should be one of the factors considered in selecting the car to rebuild. If extensive body work is necessary, obviously a car in better condition might be a wiser choice. However, if the general condition of the body is good, but there are small dents and dings here and there, the amateur should not be reluctant to try his hand. Even a large area, such as a fender or hood or door, may be repaired. In this case, however, it is always wise to graft on a used panel in good condition.

To begin any metal-straightening job, no matter how small, always try to determine the initial point of impact—that is, where the alien object first struck the metal, and in what direction it was traveling. When this is known, even vaguely, many little dents and warps can be "chased" back in the opposite direction. For instance, suppose the front fender of a Model A has been mildly crushed. Invariably, any impact on the front will cause such a fender to bow outward along the wheel-opening seam about halfway between

the front and running board. Pull on the front of the
fender, and the bulge will go back to near original
shape. This is true of all collisions. But if any hammering or metal distortion is begun at the point of impact,
some of these buckles and warps may then stay in the
metal. It's all a matter of stress.

Any damage that results in a crease probably will
require metal shrinking for repair. If an errant bumper
has put a long gouge in a fender panel, the metal along
this impact line will be stretched. In essence, there is
more metal than you need. As the gouge is worked out
with a hammer and dolly (the use of both can best be
learned by watching a body man in action), the
stretched part will leave a dimple or raised knot in the
panel. This high surface must be shrunk to the general
panel level.

Shrinking consists of heating a small spot in the
middle of the stretched area (where the metal has
been made thinner) and making it thicker. With a
small tip on the welding torch, heat a spot about the
size of a silver dollar directly in the center of the
stretched area to a strong cherry red (be careful not
to melt the metal). Immediately discard the torch and
strike a hard blow with the body hammer directly on
the heated spot. This will upset the metal and form a
crater. Now, while the metal is still hot, hold a dolly
against this new crater from the backside, and tap the
rim of the crater down with the hammer. Finally,
quench an area about six inches in diameter with a
water-soaked rag to draw the heat expansion from the

area. It may take a number of shrinking spots to complete a panel. If possible, practice on a junk piece of metal at least once.

It is always advisable to strike the metal as little as possible with a hammer, as this is nothing more than a deforming process. If a panel has been pushed severely out of shape, as with a front-end collision, push the panel back into shape with either a manual or hydraulic jack, again reversing the direction of impact. This simple bit of jack work will eliminate at least 50 percent of the damage wrinkles. A fender smashed at the headlight area will invariably have a wrinkled splash pan and rear panel, and probably will be pushed back into the door opening. By working in reverse of the impact direction, most of this secondary damage can be cleared up and will require only minor attention.

If possible, always replace a heavily damaged panel with either a new one (always expensive) or a used one (inexpensive). For front fenders, hood doors, and deck lid, this is a bolt-on operation. Clamshell, or removable, fenders were common on most cars through the early 1950's. Now fenders are generally an integral part of a quarter panel. If such a large panel must be replaced, check with a local body man on the location of the original factory mating seam before attempting a replacement.

Car bodies are made up of several panels, welded together and leaded. The entire top panel is usually welded to the body superstructure beneath the drip molding; the rear fenders mate at the doorpost, at the lower outside edge of the deck-lid opening, at the top line, etc.

To replace a badly damaged panel such as this, with a torch carefully cut the bad panel off near the factory seam, then trim to the seam with tin snips. In many cases, this trim cut can be made beneath a chrome strip. The replacement panel is also trimmed, and brazed or welded in position. If a convenient chrome strip is used, lap the new panel one inch *below* the original panel and pop-rivet along the length. By using such a chrome strip, the panel need not be welded along the major length, but only at the doorpost and deck-lid openings. This cuts replacement time considerably.

After welding, and sometimes after excessive damage, a panel may need leading. This is a process of filling a sunken area to the height of the surrounding metal. The secret in leading is to have clean and properly tinned metal. The surface to be filled should be cleaned with a wire brush at least one inch beyond the rim of the indentation or weld.

There are a number of leading fluxes on the market, some fluid, some powdered. As a general guide, follow the choice of your local body man. To apply the flux, warm the cleaned area, then spread the flux *thoroughly*. The flux will dissolve the oxide on the cleaned surface, and make "tinning" possible.

When the area is cleaned and flux applied, spread a small amount of lead solder on the surface, using a *soft* torch flame as with any kind of soldering. While the lead and metal surface are hot, wipe the solder with a clean rag to cover the area. If a spot does not take this tinning, it will not take the thicker lead filler, or body solder.

Putting the lead on can be a study in frustration. If the panel is horizontal, the lead may stay easily, but if a vertical area is being worked, more lead may end up on the ground than on the panel. The only solution is practice and patience. Some body lead is easier to use than others, due primarily to its metallic composition. Again, be guided by your local body shop.

When applying lead, brush a soft flame across the tinned metal surface occasionally to keep the metal warm (not hot!). Touch the flame to the end of the lead stick until it begins to sag, then quickly press the stick onto the surface. Keep this up until enough lead is on the surface to fill the dent or welded spot. Occasionally brush the flame across the deposited lead, just to keep it warm and pliable.

The lead is shaped with a wooden paddle dipped frequently in beeswax. The soft flame is passed across the lead deposit, and as the lead becomes plastic, the paddle is used to push it across the surface. Build this filler up slightly higher than the surrounding metal, and feather the edges smoothly. While paddling, if the surface becomes grainy, with a texture much like sugared chocolate fudge, it is being worked too cold.

Working with plastic, often called fiberglass, may prove easier for the amateur, but is possible only in an area where direct stress is not likely. Around edges, such as door or deck-lid openings, lead should be used.

Plastic filler has been highly refined over the past two decades and may be used successfully for many kinds of metalwork, and is particularly suitable for the patient beginner. It is applied without heat, and will not shrink or crack if properly mixed and applied. But it is imperative to get the best filler available, so rely on the parts house or paint store for guidance.

As with lead, the area to be filled must be thoroughly cleaned. The filler is generally in liquid form, and must be mixed with a quick-setting hardener just before application. Mixing must be thorough. The mixture will set within 15 to 30 minutes, so work must go along quickly. Spread the pasty mixture over the area with a wooden paddle or flexible rubber blade just as with lead. The hardener added to the filler creates heat, and after an hour, the filler will be firm enough to be cheese-grated (roughly contoured with an open-cut plastic filler file).

Shaping either lead or plastic should be done with a file until the amateur gains experience. A body grinder is faster, but can lead to big mistakes. Use the file to bring the filled surface down to the surrounding metal. Follow the filing with a good sanding with number 220 wet-or-dry sandpaper, carefully feathering the filler and painted edges. Clean the surface again to remove any oil, grease, or acid (Metal-Prep and water is a common cleaner), then spray a light coat of primer-surfacer on the patched area.

Alignment of body panels will make the difference

between a professional and an amateur job, so always take the few extra minutes to make a hood or door fit exactly. Body repair is hard work, very hard work. But it is also something that can be done by almost anyone, in the yard as well as garage. After all the hammering and pushing and pulling, file and sandpaper are the final test. If the metal is smooth, it is ready for the primer-surfacer. When this coat is dry it must be sanded with 220 or finer paper. Then, paint is next.

Painting

The quality of painting done by the amateur will have a direct effect on how good his project looks to the average person. It's like a pilot's flying ability—no one comments on anything but the landing. So it is with a rejuvenated old car. The chassis can be perfect, the brakes superior, the engine flawless; but unless the paint job is very good, the entire project is downgraded.

After all body work is completed, most of the chrome trim is removed from the body. A few pieces cannot be taken off, for one reason or another, but the rest should be removed. This extra work will save work later. Taping the trim properly is time-consuming, and although it takes only about a quarter of the time of complete removal, there are other problems. First, if you miscue with the tape, you can botch an otherwise good paint job. Second, if you take the trim off, the entire body gets painted, under trim and all. Third, wax and other types of film build up in the area around trim, and if you are not thorough with your preparation, the film will ruin the paint. And finally, it's a lot easier to prepare, paint, and finish a car that is minus trim.

In addition to the trim, take out the grille (so the cavity can be painted); remove the bumpers; remove the rubber bumpers from the hood, deck lid, and doors; and last, peel the rubber wind-lacing seal away from the doors and deck lid. Be careful, for you'll want to reuse this seal if it's still good. If not, you can put on new rubber, either the standard or universal type. If you really want to be meticulous, remove the door upholstery panels and kick panels. These are difficult to tape off, but the little extra effort is worthwhile.

Sandpaper for automotive use is available in both dry and wet-or-dry types, but for most purposes the latter is superior. The wet-or-dry paper may be used either way, and cost about ten cents per sheet, which means that you'll spend about a dollar for paper on the average job. Water lubricates the paper and keeps the pores clean, so the paper lasts much longer. Wet-or-dry is available in a variety of grits, from 180 through 600, and you'll need several sheets of different ratings—a couple of 180 grit, at least four of 220, four of 320, and later, some 600. In addition, pick up two sheets of dry number 80, which is very coarse.

The top is as good a starting place as any. Work down to the hood and deck lid before attacking the side panels. Hold a hose in one hand, keeping the metal end from making new scratches, and sand with the other. Direct a small flow of water on the work area as needed, which means a fine film of water at all times. Too much water won't hurt the sanding, but will make it messier for you. With just the right amount of water, the paper will glide without grabbing, but will have enough drag to tell you it's cutting.

The sanding pattern is extremely important and can have a drastic effect upon the finished job. Always go in one direction as much as possible, preferably lengthwise with the panel (much like the grain in wood), and never, never sand in circles. In some areas—for example, around windows—the direction must be changed to fit the circumstance. The pattern here should be straight across the grain.

When sanding by hand, keep the entire hand in contact with the surface, not just the fingertips or side of the palm. However, for specific areas, these two pressure points may be used.

After the entire area has been sanded, let it dry and check to be sure every inch has been covered. Any missed streaks or corners must be touched up.

With the biggest part of the surface sanded, attention can be directed toward the repaired areas, scratches, and chips. Getting these feather-edged properly is vital to a good finished product! This cannot be overstressed.

Feather-edging a large area, such as around a straightened place on a fender, is much simpler than work on small chipped spots. This is where those pieces of 80-grit dry sandpaper come in. To speed up the job, attach strips of the number 80 to a sanding block (or to an electric or air-powered "jitterbug" sander) and do the rough edging first. This paper will cut very fast and leave deep scratches, so use caution until you're familiar with it. Rough production paper works best when you sand along the edge of the spot, like walking around the edge of a lake.

After this initial fast cut, switch to 220 and the block, plus water, and repeat. The idea is to feather the break between paint and metal over a wide area. There will be at least two paint layers showing, the color coat and the primer-surfacer, and on older cars the number can be as high as eight or nine layers. The wider the band of each paint layer showing, the better the feather-edging job! A one-inch band is much better than a quarter-inch band. Finally, sand the feather-edged area in the direction of the overall sanding job.

Scratches are easy to remove if they are only one coat of paint thick. Just a little more localized pressure on the paper will do the job, but the "trough" should be feathered as much as possible. The little minute rock chips along the car front and around the wheel openings are harder to remove, and because of their sheer number it is best to use a sanding block or jitterbug. You can rent one of these handy gadgets for three dollars a day. When the rock chips are really numerous and deep, resort to an initial attack with number 100 paper, then follow up with the finer grits before priming. The entire area of color coat will usually be removed, but the effort is necessary.

The door jams and door edges should be washed clean of accumulated dirt and grease, then thoroughly sanded with both paper and number 00 steel wool. The steel wool gets down in all the little irregularities the paper can't reach; without it the final paint might not bond securely.

Fenders should be loosened and the fender welt removed; then sand the mating edges very carefully, especially chipped places. This is one location where shoddy preparation will show up quickly. New fender welt, which costs only twenty cents per foot, may be added after the color is on. Don't try to tape it.

At this stage of the game, a compressor is handy. One can be rented, along with the paint gun, for about eight dollars a day. You'll only need it for a day (actually much less). The compressor should be able to maintain a steady 80-pound pressure.

Build up a tank of pressure, drain the tank of any oil (the renter will show you how), then blow all the dirt and sanding residue from the car. Be especially careful to get all the little pieces in cracks around windows, windshield, hood, hinges, etc. Use a lint-free rag as you go along to clean the surface and all chrome and glass areas.

When the car is clean, tape off the trim, glass, and interior, and cover the engine and the seats with an old piece of anything handy. Tape a width of newspaper around the engine-compartment opening, and around the entire door opening. Tape off the door upholstery panels and glass molding if they haven't been removed. Keep all this paper as flat as possible, so debris can't fall in the folds and blow out later.

As you'll find, taping can be a maddening task. The best width to use on cars is ½ or ¾ inch, which costs about seventy-five cents per roll. You'll need one or two rolls for the average car. When applying the tape, work over at least an arm-length stretch, rather than in short 3- and 4-inch distances. This makes following an edge infinitely easier, and the whole job goes much faster.

When the entire car is taped, mix the primer-surfacer. Always remember that neither lacquer nor acrylic will go over enamel in color-coat form! They can only be used over a factory baked-enamel job, where the paint is dry clear through. Even baked enamel from local shops is likely to blister when covered with the hotter paints. This applies only to the color coats, and not to the primer, which will cover with no adverse effects. However, over red or maroon paint, which will bleed through a color coat, a bleeder sealer should be applied before the primer.

No matter what kind of paint will finally be used, enamel, lacquer, or acrylic, use a multipurpose primer with the appropriate thinner. Mix according to directions on the can (about two parts thinner to one part primer), and stir thoroughly. For primer, a good all-around spray-gun head will do, something like a number 30 on the DeVilbiss and number 362 on the Binks. Adjust the gun so that the spray fan is about 8 inches wide and 12 inches from the gun head. If the fan is too wide, there will be a thin spot in the middle; if it's too narrow the pattern will appear as a tight band. The fan adjustment is the top knob above the handle. The second knob is for material adjustment, and won't concern you too much at this time.

Make several practice passes on a piece of cardboard, with the compressor setting at 60 pounds constant. With the DeVilbiss, keep the gun 8 to 12 inches away from the surface; with the Binks, about 10 to 12 inches. Notice that when the paint-gun trigger is first depressed there is a moment when only air comes out. Following this, the paint comes. Practice making a smooth pass, keeping the gun a constant distance from the surface until the pass (which will average about two feet per swing) is completed. Start the pass on one side, swing horizontally to the other limit, raise or lower the gun nearly a fan width, and go back. Keep the gun parallel to the surface, so that one end of the fan isn't closer than the other.

Start with the door, hood, and deck-lid openings, spraying the primer on evenly, in smooth strokes. When these are done, allow them to dry for 10 or 15 minutes, then close the openings and start on the big outside metal.

If the paint is going on correctly, it will appear smooth and wet for just a short time after application. If it looks grainy, as if full of sand, the paint is too thick or you're holding the gun too far away from the surface. If the paint runs (you won't need anybody to tell you what this panic is!), it is too thin or you are holding the gun too close. If the patch alternates dry-wet-dry, or wet-runny-wet, your pass is not constant. And don't stay in one place too long. It's just one-two-three, one-two-three, etc.

If the gun doesn't seem to be making a constant fan, it may be clogged. If so, soak the head (which unscrews from the handle) and make sure all the little mixing holes are clear. Pour thinner through the handle part of the head (not through the air-delivery hole), and make sure the pressure-equalizing hole in the cup lid is open. When all this has been done, spray a little clear thinner through the gun to make sure it's really clean. As you use a primer gun, the primer, which is very thick anyway, tends to build up and close the cup-lid vent, so poke this open occasionally.

Primer is the necessary base for a fine paint job, so don't skimp. It takes about one gallon of unthinned primer-surfacer for the average car, so keep going around the car until you're sure you've got it well covered. Cost is $10 per gallon for the primer, $3 per gallon for thinner.

You don't need a special spray booth; you can spray primer right out in the open. Naturally, don't spray next to a building, or in a windstorm, but don't worry about overspray. Primer dries before it's five feet from the gun and can then be blown or washed off whatever it settles on. Don't spray under a tree that drips sap! Plan your time so that you're through spraying with at least two hours of sunlight left. The temperature should be at least 60 degrees or above. If you must spray in the cold winter or inside when it's raining, use special thinner (the paint store will decide for you).

After the primer has dried for 20 or 30 minutes, the tape can be removed. Although it is possible to go right ahead and sand the car (dry) and follow with the color coats of paint, it is best to allow the primer to cure for several days, even weeks. The primer will dry and shrink, so allow about four weeks' time for a good-quality job. You can drive the car meanwhile.

Scratches don't come from the paint can or from the gun, they are caused by improper sanding. So, take it easy during the primer-sanding operation. The thoroughly dried primer will sand easily with either dry or wet paper, and it is advisable to use either a 320 or 400 grit. Remember this is the base for the color, and coarser paper will leave scratches too deep for the color paint to cover.

Next, use the wax- and grease-remover solution, completely washing the car, even the tiniest cracks. This is vital, for any foreign substance will invariably ruin an otherwise perfect job. For instance, just the marks left by your fingers will leave dark splotches under the final color. When washing the car with the cleaning solution, always use clean, lint-free rags (don't use shop towels, as they often are cleaned with low-grade solvents that contain contaminants which reduce paint adhesion). It is wise to use the special cleanser always, but in a pinch you can use lacquer thinner, applied with a very wet rag and immediately wiped off with a dry rag. Don't wait even a minute if you use thinner, as it is "hot" and will quickly soften the surfacer and may cause other damage below.

The car is now ready for the final color, and this is the time most amateur painters get the jitters. It is also the time when one step must follow the other in rapid succession, so having the procedures well established in your mind will insure best results.

What you do from now on depends a lot upon the paint you use; the type, not the brand. Lacquer is the easiest to spray for the novice, followed by acrylic, then enamel. Lacquer and acrylic dry much faster, compensating for many application errors. Or at least, for a few.

A note about the spraying environment. It is often possible to rent the facilities of a paint shop over the weekend, thereby gaining the equipment and the paint booth. However, the only real requirement is that enamel must be painted in a dust-free atmosphere. A fly on the surface can also create a mess. Don't paint enamel inside your family garage, unless you don't mind an overspray on everything. Enamel overspray will stay, while lacquer and acrylic will dust or wash away. Lacquer and acrylic can be sprayed quite well outdoors.

Basically, paint is a mixture of pigments (coloring matter) and a binder; the latter merely holds the pigment particles together. Usually made from inorganic matter, pigment can be mixed with many other elements and compounds, from bronze to gold, to silver powder, etc.

The thinner, a vital partner to paint, is the real paint base and makes drying possible. Obviously the thinner also lowers the viscosity of the paint so the solution can be sprayed through a gun.

The color coat is sprayed exactly like the primer-surfacer. However, some extra preparation might be needed if lacquer or acrylic is being applied over enamel. Just as a precaution, if the old paint is enamel, spray a coat of DuPont No. 22 sealer on the primer-surfacer. This will keep the enamel from raising owing to the hot lacquer thinner. If you're not sure, always spray a test patch first, but a sealer is the best bet.

Because you're spraying a panel at a time, you must get in the habit of spraying consistently. Don't put paint on heavily in one area and lightly in another. As you start a panel, begin each stroke slightly in from the edge, and stop slightly short. Then, as the next panel is painted, the overspray from both strokes will combine to give the right amount of coverage. This will take time to learn.

The biggest single problem the amateur faces is stroke inconsistency. The paint must overlap every-where; otherwise it will appear streaked when it dries. It might be advisable for the beginner to make hori-zontal strokes on the panel first, follow with vertical strokes (with the gun laid on its side to keep the fan pattern consistent), and finish with crisscross strokes. The idea is to get the same amount of paint every-where.

If lacquer is being used, you can paint merrily on

your way. However, acrylic must be allowed to "flash," that is, surface-harden, before the next coat is applied. Following the enamel procedure works well with acrylic. Enamel, being a very slow drier, cannot be applied all at once. The first time around the car, a very light, or tack, coat is applied. This will become sticky in a few minutes and helps make subsequent spraying easier by increasing adhesion. The second coat of enamel is sprayed normally. The amateur should never try to get all the paint (two gallons required for the average car) on the car in one pass.

Starting with the top, spray each stroke evenly. If you load up a particular area, which is easy to do, expect a run. But don't panic, just continue with the job, and ease off on the amount of paint. When the first cover coat is finished, dip a tiny brush in enamel thinner and remove as much of the sag (run) excess as possible. Try to soak up the excess, not spread it around. When the excess is removed, very gingerly fog a little paint over the area. If you do the job well, the little boo-boo won't be apparent (good painters completely eradicate the run). On the next coat, go easy in this area, again just lightly fogging over the top.

Usually, an enamel job requires three passes—the tack coat, first color, and second color. After the last coat, wait a couple of minutes, check for sags and repair them, then leave the car to dry overnight. In fact, since enamel should be painted indoors, leave the car for a couple of days before detailing if possible.

A note about enamel and moisture. Moisture and

paint just don't mix, so if you wash the floor to keep dust down, let it dry before you start painting. This might be a good time to discuss temperature and paint. Temperatures shouldn't be under 60 or over 100 degrees Fahrenheit when you paint; otherwise special steps are required. This is the temperature of the metal, which may be different than the temperature of the environment. If you're painting lacquer or acrylic out in the backyard, that hot sun can make the body sizzle.

Special additives are available to control drying time, such as DuPont No. 3656 (rather than normal 366/g) for acrylic, which will slow the drying process if the temperature is too hot. If the weather is wet or cold, the color can "blush"; that is, moisture is trapped in the paint, so a slower thinner or special retarder might be needed. The local paint salesman will guide you here. At all times, follow the mixing directions of the manufacturer exactly!

Although the enamel job can be done all at one spraying, lacquer and acrylic require more elapsed time for the best job. If you have the time, spray the latter in several good coats, then allow to dry for a couple of days. Wet-sand with 600 sandpaper, then spray with several more coats. Whereas enamel doesn't require any after-spray special attention, lacquer and acrylic must be color-sanded with 600 paper before final rubbing out with rubbing compound.

10 Upholstery

Once in a great while, an old car will come along with paint in excellent condition, tires good for another 20,-000 miles, and upholstery as fine as new. Most of us, though, never make such a find. We do everything the hard way, including work seldom considered fit for the amateur, such as upholstery. However, stitching up new upholstery is perhaps the least demanding aspect of fixing up any car, young or old. All it takes is planning, and bushels of patience.

Only three types of material were generally used in automotive upholstery prior to 1950—cotton, mohair, and leather. Synthetic materials have since completely dominated the field, and a modern car may have a combination of nylon (or similar synthetic) and Naugahyde. These new materials are far superior to their aged counterparts. They wear better and should be considered for any upholstery replacement.

Until the mid-1950's it was common practice to cover door panels, seats, and the roof area with a natural fabric such as woven cotton, which was easy to stretch taut. For some vague reason, almost no attention was paid to upholstery durability or life expectancy.

Any car built before 1955, especially prior to 1949, will probably suffer from poor upholstery, so poor in fact that repair is not feasible. It is better to put a new covering on everything. But use caution! Never rip out the old panels haphazardly and throw them in the trash. Instead, remove every piece of cloth carefully, without tearing if possible, and save for patterns.

If the car is fitted with a headliner, this liner will be supported across the top by hidden metal bows and attached at the sides by tacks beneath the wind lacing. The door and kick panels will be secured by visible or hidden screws or clips, and the seat covers will be pinned to the cushion springs by bent wire "hog rings." It will take approximately three hours to strip a four-door sedan such as a 1954 Plymouth.

Whenever there are more than two distinct pieces in a panel of upholstery, such as a headliner, number the parts with chalk for later reference.

The choice of new upholstery material is strictly personal, but will probably be tempered by price. Genuine leather is exotic but tremendously expensive. Enough for that Plymouth will cost almost $300! A bit steep. Mohair, that sophisticated material very similar to velvet, is also expensive, and not really comfortable or durable. Newer synthetics of this type are better and much less costly. Obviously the older cottons are out. That leaves the friezes and Naugahydes, both excellent and relatively inexpensive. The frieze material is like quality cotton or wool, but durable. Its great fault is susceptibility to soiling. Naugahyde, a synthetic leather, is the most durable and soil-resistant, but susceptible to temperature changes.

Unless a car is being restored to authentic condition, either frieze or Naugahyde will be the best material. Of the two, the first is easier to sew and install, the latter more "custom."

Although only Naugahyde and leather require a special long-stitch upholstery sewing machine, it is advisable to secure such a machine if possible. This may be difficult in the smallest village, but many upholsterers (they don't have to be automotive) will rent or loan a machine. And don't overlook the high-school sewing class, which usually has such a machine. If the ordinary sewing machine is used, the stitch pattern may be too close, so the needle acts more like a knife than a needle, and some of these home machines will not take heavy material. Always use the best quality upholstery thread available, preferably nylon. Otherwise the thread will wear and break prematurely.

Practice sewing on the machine before starting the real job, and pay close attention to making long, straight stitch lines. Uneven stitches in upholstery show up like a sore thumb. This, more than anything else, is the difference between the very good and the so-so upholsterer.

Perhaps the first thing to attempt should be the headliner. This is the biggest single piece, but probably the simplest to make. Cut the headliner apart at the seams, cutting the thread and not the material. With each separate panel as a pattern, cut new panels at least half an inch larger around the border. They will be trimmed later. When the new panels are cut, stitch them together on the pattern of the original. This will require just one straight simple seam. Note, however, that the metal headliner bows were fitted in little "tubes" sewn over this seam, on the backside. Make new tubes and sew them onto the new headliner. In some headliners the number of individual panels may vary from two to five.

When the sewing is finished, insert the metal bows in the cloth tubes, then insert the bows in the top sockets. Now begins the careful work. Pull the front and back of the liner taut and tack in place. Use just one or two tacks at either end for now. Then do the same at several points along the sides, working in sections almost as though you were tack-welding a metal panel. As the liner is pulled tight, areas that need re-alignment will show up. Keep pulling tighter until the headliner is taut everywhere, even in the corners. When this is accomplished, there will be excess material to trim from the sides. Where the liner must bend around a corner, such as under window garnish moldings, the material should be snipped with scissors to make the forming smooth.

New wind lacing may be made up with upholstery material and rubber "rope" and tacked in place around the door openings, effectively hiding the headliner edges and forming a wind seal for the door cracks.

The door panels will be a bit harder. When the original upholstery is removed from the soft board backing, the old backing may disintegrate. It can be replaced by new board, which is quite inexpensive. Most door and kick panels are held to the metal by hidden clips. These clips must be in good condition and installed in any new board before the upholstery material as attached.

Again use the original material as a pattern and make your cuts at least half an inch oversize. Panels are normally a single piece without ornate stitching or pleats. However, to get a much better and richer-looking job, it is possible to insert a sheet of thin cotton batting between the material and a piece of backing cotton. When the material is then secured to the board, it has a full look.

At the bottom of these panels, it is common practice to include a 5- to 7-inch strip of carpeting as scuff protection. If this is done, the carpeting should be trimmed with a piece of matching Naugahyde, then sewn to the main panel. The panel edges are lapped over the backing board and stapled in place. Wrinkles are removed as with the headliner. As a secondary bond of material to board, an ordinary cement may be used.

Covering the seats is the hardest job, because the seams must be very straight to give the best appearance. As with the door panels and headliner, use the original as a guide. When an original is not available, it is best to call on the professional for limited help—at least to create and sew up the new panel.

It is very important to rebuild the seat platforms if they are damaged, which is usually the case. Cotton used as padding may be pushed out of place, big holes may be worn in the padding, and often the springs will need to be replaced or repaired. All this takes little time and has a direct effect on the finished product.

New cotton or foam-rubber padding should be purchased in large sheets, enough to cover each seat bottom and back completely, then trimmed to size. But be careful to use just enough padding. Too much makes the seats bulky and uncomfortable. Half an inch of padding, whether cotton or foam rubber, is about maximum.

The seat covers are pulled taut as the headliner was, and the edges secured to the wire springs by new hog rings. The amateur tends to make seat covers too loose, so don't be afraid to pull on the material.

Carpeting is a matter of duplicating whatever shape is on the floor, but substituting newer and better materials. For the best result, always trim the carpeting, and glue any vertical pieces, for example those fit against the firewall. Always put a good thick piece of carpet backing on the floor as insulation.

Making up the tuck and roll upholstery panels so popular with custom car fans is a study in patience, but something most first-timers can accomplish with care. Remember that a tuck and roll segment is not made by sewing visable seams down a panel of material.

When tuck and roll is attempted, the outside material is separated from a quality backing material by foam rubber (never cotton). The first step is to turn the outside material on its face, then lay out a series of parallel lines on the back side, from one to three inches apart, depending on how wide the pleats are to be.

At the sewing machine, the backing material is covered by a half-inch sheet of quality foam. Next, the outside material is laid on the foam, then folded back right or left to the first marked line, with the face of the material together. A stitch is then run down this folded edge. The procedure is repeated across the panel, so that when the new panel is viewed from the front, the stitch is tucked under and invisible. This piece of tuck and roll is then trimmed like any other piece of material and included in the upholstery job.

Cleaning upholstery is especially important. It keeps new upholstery new, and makes old upholstery last longer. There are a number of special cleansers on the market, all workable. The only place extra caution must be observed is the old headliner. It is susceptible to tearing under the slightest pressure and is prone to lose its fuzz when rubbed.

There are also several upholstery "painting" kits available. These will at least help tired upholstery, but don't expect such a dye or paint to substitute for the real thing.

11 The Tool Box

You can't be a good doctor without the right instruments, nor can you expect to do good work on a car with just a screwdriver and a pair of pliers. It may take years for the amateur mechanic to build up a proper cross section of automotive tools, but the investment will be repaid a hundred times over.

Once in a while, a lucky youngster is given a small fortune in hand and power tools, usually as hand-me-downs from a mechanic father. More often, he must start from scratch and purchase each tool as money allows. Sometimes, this can be a costly experience. It is easy to overbuy—to buy the wrong kind of wrench, to duplicate unnecessarily, to spend tool dollars unwisely. Having a toolbox full of the right kind of wrenches is important. It is possible to make do with lesser tools, but the results in time and workmanship show the shortage.

It is almost impossible to equip the home garage without a good firsthand knowledge of basic hand tools, and at least a rudimentary acquaintance with power equipment. For this reason, store-window enthusiasm should never precede experience. In the beginning, tools can be limited; as mechanical ability improves, so will the tool selection and diversification. For a beginning, a cash outlay of between $15 and $25 may be considered average, and only a small fraction of what the ultimate toolbox will cost. But for these few dollars, enough tools can be purchased to make 95 percent of all automotive repairs.

The initial tool-buying schedule should include a wide assortment of combination wrenches (the common box- and open-end design) ranging in size from the small ⅜ to at least 1 inch. Small and medium size crescents will be invaluable additions, especially for the few very large bolts and nuts, usually found on the chassis or suspension. A small pipe wrench will also be necessary in many cases, to be used as a portable vise.

A good assortment of screwdrivers is vital. In flat blades, you will want at least two small tips (the very tiny tips for small screw slots), with one short and one long shank. The same holds true for Phillips-head 'drivers. Medium-sized screwdrivers in both Phillips and flat-head design will be used 80 percent of the time, but always have a big flat screwdriver available for the stubborn jobs. The simplest toolbox, then, would have at least seven screwdrivers.

Continuing with the supereconomy tool chest, a good ball-peen hammer is essential, along with a six-inch cold chisel and a tapered punch. Pliers can be limited to one pair at first. A hacksaw, with several extra blades, and a retractable tape measure round out the basic assortment. Assuming that all these individual pieces of equipment must be purchased new, the price can vary from the aforementioned $15 low to as much as $50! This is where the wise shopping comes in.

"All tools are alike." Or so a popular misconception goes. The fact is, tools of similar design, and even items that look exactly alike, can be vastly different. The difference is primarily in service and life. The more expensive the tool, as a general rule, the better it will serve over an extended period of heavy use. Because of this important quality factor, a professional will need, and use, tools far more expensive than the amateur will ever require. A good example of this is the $\frac{1}{2}$-inch combination wrench. The $\frac{1}{2}$- and $\frac{9}{16}$-inch sizes are probably the most used wrenches in a toolbox. If the professional uses such a wrench every day for one month, this is roughly equivalent to two years of amateur use. The less expensive tool will not be made of the better alloys, nor will the manufacturing techniques be as sophisticated. However, although the professional might get only two months' hard usage from such a wrench, the amateur can expect several years of trouble-free service.

This, then, is the secret to buying tools. If nothing more than an automotive hobby is anticipated, the less costly tools will be fine. If a career in mechanics is considered, it would be wise to begin stockpiling the better brands early, thus spreading the cost over a wide period of time.

Choosing the brand of hand tool to buy will always be a personal matter, but the best guideline remains the local professional mechanics. When a qualified mechanic buys a wrench, he expects it to work properly for a long period of time. And he also expects competent, immediate service on the tool, if necessary. For this reason, the better manufacturers keep traveling service representatives on the road throughout the year, taking tool sales directly to the shop and repairing damaged tools as necessary.

The amateur should not overlook the tools normally sold by the local auto-parts store, for these will range in price from inexpensive to costly. Often, there will be special sales on tools, particularly on ratchet-socket sets. Mail-order stores such as Sears and Montgomery Ward carry a full line of quality tools well suited to either the amateur or professional. They also offer an excellent incentive—if a tool breaks or wears out, replacement or repair is immediate.

By keeping close tabs on the newspaper advertisements, especially in towns with a population of 15,000 or more, some excellent used tools can be purchased at a fraction of the new price. Usually, when used tools are bought, they can be purchased piecemeal or in a complete set. It is always wise to buy the whole set, if possible, since the price for an average complete rollaway full of used equipment will run well under $100. A new rollaway will cost from $50 to $200, and used ones are hard to find. At the same time, someone selling a set of tools will generally include a few power tools, such as a drill and grinder.

There is one avenue for tool procurement that should never be overlooked, and it solves some pressing family problems at the same time. Tools make excellent gifts, especially if you are receiving them. The boy over fifteen years old is very difficult to buy presents for, but if the family and friends know how important tools are, it takes very few birthdays and other special occasions to outfit the garage. Don't be vague about what is needed. Write it down and be sure you get the right "surprise."

Power tools are more specialized than hand tools, and should be selected more carefully. Brand name is not nearly so important, but continuing service is. Should the power tool malfunction, it is nice to have a repair shop handy. The selection of power equipment will probably be dictated by sheer cost, but every mechanic needs a basic group. This will include a good ¼-inch drill (⅜-inch is bigger and better, but also more expensive), a complete set of drill bits, a soldering gun, a bench grinder, and an electric trouble light.

All power equipment over and above this selection will be a convenience, but will have a definite effect on the quality of work done on automobiles. For instance, if extensive body and fender work is anticipated, a body power grinder is very necessary. (It will double as a paint polisher.) But this is a long-term investment at the new cost of nearly $150 (used grinders can be bought from shops for around $25). An air compressor is extremely handy around the home workshop, costing upward of $150 new ($25 used). An electric or air-impact wrench must definitely be included in the serious amateur's toolbox, and will cost a bundle. Such a power tool is vital if an efficient automotive repair career is contemplated.

Other work-saving tools are the drill press, which costs about $150 new ($40 used); and the small combination wood-metal band saw, $150 new ($25 used). These are really luxuries, but will find use in all kinds of home-equipment repairs (furniture, appliances, etc.).

Maintenance of tools, both hand and power, will determine how long they last. Organization of the tool-box or wall rack is the first item on the agenda. Whenever a tool is left out of place, chances are good it will be lost. Serious mechanics make a habit of returning all tools to their proper place as soon as a job is complete, and at the end of each day.

Clean tools are a personal matter but reflect directly on the work of a career mechanic. If a mechanic keeps a clean area and wipes all his tools clean after a job, chances are his attention to the repair job will be good. A sloppy mechanic will have sloppy tools.

Hand tools don't require more than cleaning, but power equipment must be inspected every time it is used. The usual problem with a power tool is deterioration of the electrical cord. These cords should be replaced at the first sign of wear or breaking, and always with wire as good as the original. Power-tool failures are also due to the malfunction of simple parts. Common for drills are worn brushes, and perhaps armature bushings. Such problems can easily be handled by the home mechanic, saving many dollars on a repair bill.

Whether a toolbox is necesasry is a personal opinion, but such a box certainly aids in tool organization. The rollaway box, fitted with casters, is the most common and may have two or more drawers. A body-and-fender repairman tends to buy the two-drawer model with a large lower storage space for hammers, dollies, power grinder, etc. The motor mechanic doesn't need such a big bottom storage area, so may have three, four, or even six drawers in the cabinet. A smaller portable toolbox set atop the rollaway cabinet is added as the mechanic becomes more specialized.

12 When You're Stuck with a Problem

As in politics, so in automotive repair, nearly everyone can give free advice on a problem. Also as in politics, much of the advice has little value. Still, when you're stumped with a mechanical question, you've got to ask someone for help. Books can go just so far; after that you must rely on personal questions and answers.

The best place to go for automotive advice is to a man who makes car repair his profession. But there is a time and place to ask questions. During a professional man's spare time, avoid shop talk like the plague. Instead, ask the mechanic during his normal work hours, but at a time when he can answer without interruption of his normal work. For instance, the ideal time for a short question-and-answer period is during the morning or afternoon coffee break. Better yet, if you need information that takes a little explaining, such as pointers on automatic transmissions or engine assembly, and if you have at least a casual acquaintance with the mechanic, try asking over lunch.

Most professional mechanics are proud of their work and the special skills they have acquired, and are more than willing to pass answers along. They will be especially helpful if you can arrange to visit with them during the time they are actually working on a job similar to yours. For instance, if you want to know about rear ends, arrange to visit the local garage and watch as the mechanic works on a differential. He can then explain in detail what he is doing, generally with far better results than if he must rely on words alone.

At the same time, be prepared to ask intelligent questions. The mechanic must take for granted your basic knowledge of automotive engineering. He doesn't expect an expert, but when he speaks of this or that part, he expects you to have a reasonable idea of what it is and where it fits.

It is wise to bone up on your particular car as much as possible. There won't be much information available on a 1939 Plymouth, but there will be a good deal of printed matter on a 1949 Ford. Of course, the logical place to start is the automobile agency. Ask for any old sales literature available, then spend time in the library looking through old automotive magazines and repair manuals. Two hours spent in a library will be repaid hundreds of times during actual work.

Bear in mind that many mechanics are specialists, and their particular experience may be limited to specific automobiles or parts of cars. A mechanic who has tor will often allow after-school hours and, in special cases, even make certain parts of the rebuilding a class project. Often you can break a project up into segments and do each at the most advantageous place.

For instance, if a 1953 Chevrolet is being rebuilt, the engine and transmisison can be removed and worked on during class and after school. The rest of the car can be taken home so that extra time can be spent on making the chassis and body ready for the renovated engine. In this way, the entire project will seem to take much less time to complete.

It is not advisable to write to automotive magazines with questions about rebuilding your particular car, simply because the magazine staff cannot possibly answer all the daily mail on such subjects. The enthusiast publications normally have one or two technical editors, and all mail is answered in the magazine's question-and-answer column. The editors select a cross section of mail on the most popular questions, but seldom answer with a personal reply.

Finally, little correspondence is ever answered by the automobile factories unless it is relative to performance of their newer cars. As an example, Ford Motor Company has retained one of the best race-car builders to answer questions on their new cars, but makes no effort to answer mail concerning older Fords.

Appendix 1

Sources for Car Parts

The most useful lists any amateur mechanic can have are the sources of supply or information concerning old cars. Included below are places where parts for old cars (anything more than three years old) can be purchased. Appendix 2 gives addresses of special car clubs located throughout the United States. The latter are especially helpful when information or parts for rebuilding an old car are difficult to find. Club addresses change periodically, but in most cases the mail is forwarded.

ARIZONA

Antique Auto Parts & Upholstery
2015 N. Scottsdale Rd.
Scottsdale, Ariz.:
Tops and trim made to original specifications, and material for same.

183

CALIFORNIA

Roy's Auto Painting & Body Works
5004 Calmview Ave.
Baldwin Park, Calif.:
   Paint specialists for antique and classic cars.

Bellflower Auto Trim
9724 Alondra Blvd.
Bellflower, Calif.:
   Upholstery, trim, tops made to order.

Classic Parts
17920 Clark Ave.
Bellflower, Calif.:
   Model A, T, and other early parts; home of "Velvet
   Power" motor mounts.

Garber & Sons
Box 52
Bijou, Calif.:
   Wheels repaired and made to order—all types.

Automotive, Etc.
6306 Beach Blvd.
Buena Park, Calif.:
   New and used parts for Fords and other old makes.

Lucas Engineering
Box 174
Culver City, Calif.:
   Reproduction "Aermore" exhaust whistles; also parts for
   several vintage makes. Free catalogue.

Lewis C. Malucci
9810 E. Garvey
El Monte, Calif.:
   Buys and sells Model A cars and parts.

Bunch's Auto Parts
Rt. 3, Box 1620
Escalon, Calif.:
   Used parts for many early cars. Query.

Classic Car Parts
19020 Anelo St.
Gardena, Calif.:
   Very complete line of parts for all classics.

Egge Machine Co.
136 E. Alondra St.
Gardena, Calif.:
   Pistons, other parts for 1900 and later Chevrolet, Nash,
   Dodge, Plymouth, Ford, and others.

Sheldon Greenland
3761 Hillway Dr.
Glendale, Calif.:
   Ford patent plates, oilers, hubcaps, much more.

Ford Obsolete of Hollywood
5001 Hollywood Blvd.
Hollywood, Calif.:
   Complete stock of parts for Fords, 1928–48.

Harry Pulfer
2700 Mary St.
La Crescenta, Calif.:
   Nameplates, brass scripts, enameled medallions for all
   old cars. Free price lists

Antique Car Book Co.
Box 311
La Mirada, Calif.:
    Reprinted owner manuals, shop guides for 1915–48 cars.
    Free price list.

Ed & Jim's Garage
3714 E. 4th St.
Long Beach, Calif.:
    Rebuilt engines for Models A and T, others.

Fred Stiver
1030 Rilma Lane
Los Altos, Calif.:
    Reproduction Model T radiators and cooling parts.

A-M Parts Mfg. Co.
1814 S. Grand Ave.
Los Angeles, Calif.:
    Engine parts made to order, all old cars.

Ford Parts Obsolete Inc.
616 E. Florence Ave.
Los Angeles, Calif.:
    New and used parts for T, A, and V8's.

Motor Bearing Service Inc.
2100 S. Grand Ave.
Los Angeles, Calif.:
    Crankshafts ground, bearings rebabbitted.

Precision Brass Division
Associated Steel Co.
1700 Sawtelle Blvd.
Los Angeles, Calif.:
    New brass brackets, handles, robe rails.

Mal's "A" Sales
4968 S. Pacheco Blvd.
Martinez, Calif.:
    Complete line new and used Ford parts, 1921–41.

Ford Parts & Accessories
829 E. 2nd St.
National City, Calif.:
    Used parts, mostly Model A and V8.

Ford Duplicators Co.
8046 Lankershim Blvd.
N. Hollywood, Calif.:
    Fiberglass body and other metal items, 1909–67 Ford.
    Catalogue, $1.

Vintage Paint Co.
Box 2153
Oakland, Calif.:
    Authentic duplicate colors for all antiques.

Ken Sorenson Top Shop
38 N. Hill Ave.
Pasadena, Calif.:
    1911–27 Model T tops.

Model A Parts & Accessories
612 El Camino Real
Redondo Beach, Calif.:
    Complete line of parts, Ford 1928–41.

Antique Auto Parts Inc.
9113 E. Garvey Blvd.
Rosemead, Calif.:
    Large stock, A, T, and later Ford parts.

Moulded Products Co.
9107 E. Garvey Blvd.
Rosemead, Calif.:
    Molded rubber parts for Model A Fords.

Obsolete Ford Parts
3426 Rio Linda Blvd.
Sacramento, Calif.:
    Complete line of old Ford parts, new and used.

Vintage Auto Center
3210 S. Bascom
San Jose, Calif.:
    Some parts for most vintage and classic cars.

Vintage Auto Parts
1023 E. 4th St.
Santa Ana, Calif.:
    Many parts for Ford and others.

Andy's Auto Center
1685 Old Mission Road
S. San Francisco, Calif.:
    A, T, and early V8 parts.

McClure's Antique Auto Parts
2216 S. Pontius Ave.
W. Los Angeles, Calif.:
    1920–40 parts for Ford, Dodge, Chevrolet, others.

COLORADO

Gaslight Auto Parts Western Inc.
2190 S. Raritan
Denver, Colo.:
    Complete line parts for antique cars only.

Chris Music
122 W. Laurel
Ft. Collins, Colo.:
   Auto brass restored.

CONNECTICUT

A & L Parts Specialties
Drawer 82
Bloomfield, Conn.:
   A, B, and T parts.

Amato's Inc.
420 Main St.
Middletown, Conn.:
   Model T parts in large quantity.

Lebov Brothers
400 Boulevard
New Haven, Conn.:
   Brass refinishing.

FLORIDA

Jim's Auto Parts
Box 933
S. Miami, Fla.:
   Parts for various vintage, classic cars.

GEORGIA

Antique Auto Museum
2045 Robson Place, N.E.
Atlanta, Ga.:
   Miscellaneous parts for miscellaneous old cars.

Obsolete Ford Parts Co.
102 W. Marion Ave.
Nashville, Ga.:
    T, A, early V8 parts, 1928–48. Catalogue, 50¢.

ILLINOIS

Smitty's Cut & Cover Shop
211 E. 8th St.
Beardstown, Ill.:
    Install-it-yourself tops and upholstery for old cars.

All Ford Parts International
336 W. 63rd St.
Chicago, Ill.:
    1909–37 Ford parts.

Amsco Parts Manufacturing Co.
1608 S. Wabash Ave.
Chicago, Ill.:
    Replacement parts and accessories.

Faber Schneider Radiator Co.
2450 S. Wabash Ave.
Chicago, Ill.:
    New Model T radiators.

J. C. Whitney Co.
1917 Archer Ave.
Chicago, Ill.:
    Miscellaneous parts for Fords and other old cars.

Syverson Cabinet Co.
3036 Orchard Place
Des Plaines, Ill.:
    Wooden parts that "Fit to a T."

Hank's Vintage Ford Parts
735 N. 14th St.
Quincy, Ill.:
  Early Ford parts, 1909–31. Catalogue, 10¢.

IOWA

Atmor Corporation
Box 422
Hampton, Iowa:
  New crankshafts for Model T Fords.

KANSAS

Welsh Antique Auto Parts Store
Route 3
Junction City, Kan.:
  Various antique and classic parts—most makes.

MARYLAND

Montgomery Ward & Co.
Baltimore, Md.:
  Engine and other parts for old Fords, others.

MASSACHUSETTS

LaBaron Bonney Co.
10 Bridge St.
Haverhill, Mass.:
  Model A upholstering materials; cloth, pads, panels, tops.

"Top Brass"
516 Country Lane
Louisville, Mass.:
  Brass horn and lamp repair.

MICHIGAN

John F. Kolar Assoc.
265 Hunter Blvd.
Birmingham, Mich.:
    Makes and repairs cloisonné enamel emblems.
Kenneth E. Binder
9530 Woodside
Detroit, Mich.:
    Early upholstery materials, tops, seats.
Spinster Corporation
22473 Cora St.
Farmington, Mich.:
    Model A shock absorbers and suspension parts.
Robert C. Burchill
4150-24th Ave.
Pt. Huron, Mich.:
    Model A and T parts.

MINNESOTA

Motor Age Company
Box 6
Long Lake, Minn.:
    New motor meters for all early cars.
Aged Auto Parts Company
1411-13th Ave. N.
Minneapolis, Minn.:
    New oak top kits for 1928–36 Fords and others.
Little Dearborn Parts
2015 Washington Ave. N.
Minneapolis, Minn.:
    Early Ford parts.

Royce D. Peterson
431 Layman Lane
Minneapolis, Minn.:
    Manufactures new Model T parts.

MISSOURI

Bill Fessler
1517 McGee St.
Kansas City, Mo.:
    Top and upholstery materials.

Leo's Model T Repair
911 E. 18th St.
Kansas City, Mo.:
    Remanufactured engine parts, Ford 1909–31.

NEW JERSEY

William Farhy
866 Allwood Dr.
Clifton, N.J.:
    Model T and A parts.

Lackawana Leather Co.
Hackettstown, N.J.:
    Leather for reupholstering all vintage cars.

Mark Auto Co. Inc.
Layton, N.J.:
    Model T and A parts.

Stitt Mfg. & Supply Co.
2771 Brunswick Pike
Trenton, N.J.:
    Upholstery and tops made for all old cars.

Ted Kessler
317 N. Ogden St.
Buffalo, N.Y.:
    Parts for early V8 Fords.

Automotive Obsolete
43–71-156th St.
Flushing, N.Y.:
    Model A parts exclusively. Catalogue, 25¢.

Vintage Car Store
Nyack, N.Y.:
    Mostly sells restored classics; some parts.

Long Island Auto Museum
Museum Square
Southampton, L.I., N.Y.:
    Parts for various old makes, mostly T.

Firestone Tire & Rubber Co.
Akron, Ohio:
    New tires in most sizes.

Jim Schmidt
916 State Road
Hickley, Ohio:
    Ford nuts, bolts, trim screws, small parts.

M. H. Martin Company
1118 Lincoln Way E.
Massillon, Ohio:
    Rubber floormats for Model T and others.

Donald H. Snyder
New Springfield, Ohio:
   Seat spring units.

Gaslight Auto Parts
Box 291
Urbana, Ohio:
   Parts for antique cars.

OKLAHOMA

Russell Jones
c/o Jack Bowker Sales
Ponca City, Okla.:
   New and used parts for Lincoln, Mercury, Ford.

PENNSYLVANIA

Klein Kars
E. Ann Klein St.
Elizabethtown, Pa.:
   New tires for old cars.

Swigart Assoc. Inc.
409 Penn St.
Huntington, Pa.:
   Specializes in insurance for antique cars.

Consula Wood Wheels
Box 143
Mechanicsburg, Pa.:
   Wheels repaired and made to order.

Sears Roebuck and Co.
Roosevelt Blvd.
Philadelphia, Pa.:
   Parts for early Fords and other makes.

Speedometer Service Co.
4740 Baum Blvd.
Pittsburgh, Pa.:
   Old speedometers sold and repaired.

J. C. Taylor
55 Long Lane
Upper Darby, Pa.:
   Insurance for antique cars.

Hoopes Bros. & Darlington
E. Market St.
West Chester, Pa.:
   Rebuilt wooden wheels on your rims.

Palmer's Reproduction
700 W. King St.
York, Pa.:
   Model A sheetmetal panels.

RHODE ISLAND

Bill's Auto Parts
Valley Fall, R.I.:
   Wide selection of parts for antiques and classics.

SOUTH CAROLINA

Harry Gregory
1930 Surrey St.
Columbia, S.C.:
   Reproductions of some Ford floor and body items.

TENNESSEE

Coulter Ford Haven
Sevierville Road
Maryville, Tenn.:
   New and used Ford parts.

TEXAS

Babb's Custom Automotive
1241 Walnut St.
Abilene, Tex.:
   Early Ford V8 body parts; also A and B items.

Howell's Antique Car Shop
1090 Linberg Drive
Beaumont, Tex.:
   Mostly Ford, but also other old car parts.

Sheet Metal Products
Box 1469
Beaumont, Tex.:
   Body, chassis, engine parts.

VIRGINIA

Clearbrook Wollen Shop
Clearbrook, Va.:
   Upholstery cloth for late T and A closed cars.

WISCONSIN

Ernie Anderson
2626 Lincoln Ave.
LaCrosse, Wis.:
   Brass switch plates, under-door panels for Model T's.

B. W. Wisniewski Inc.
203 W. Maple St.
Milwaukee, Wis.:
   Parts for all makes of popular cars.

Appendix 2

Special Car Clubs

American Austin-Bantam Club
P.O. Box 328
Morris, N.Y.

American Hot Rod Association
1820 W. 91st Place
Kansas City, Mo.

Antique Automobile Club
Hershey Museum
Hershey, Pa.

Auburn-Cord-Duesenberg Club
202 Lawton Dr.
Milpitas, Calif.

Buick Collectors Club
4730 Centre Ave.
Pittsburgh, Pa. 15213

Cadillac-LaSalle Club
22600 Amherst St.
St. Claire Shores, Mich.

Classic Car Club of America
114 Liberty St.
New York 6, N.Y.

Corvette Club
P.O. Box 473
Pasadena, Calif.

Crosley Owners Club
W. T. Palmer
645 N. Howard St.
Akron 10, Ohio

Curved Dash Olds Club
Attn.: James Staats
Kilty Dr.
New Hope, Pa.

Formula Racing Assn.
2900 W. Magnolia Blvd.
Burbank, Calif.

Four-Wheel Drive Assn.
Walker Bank Building
Salt Lake City 11, Utah

Franklin Automobile Club
P.O. Box 535
Cumberland, Md.

Golden Lions CHRYSLER Club
909 Edgewood Terrace
Wilmington, Del. 19809

Haynes-Apperson Club
610 S. Webster St.
Kokomo, Ind.

Horseless Carriage Club
9031 E. Florence Ave.
Downey, Calif.

Hudson Super Six Club
1118 N. Alton Ave.
Indianapolis, Ind. 46222

Hupmobile-Graham Club
609 Cherry St.
Winnetka, Ill.

Hupp Owners Club
P.O. Box 328
Mansfield, Ohio

ISCARA (Sports Cars)
Lew Leslie
4107 Los Feliz Blvd.
Los Angeles 27, Calif.

Isotta-Fraschini Club
1755 Sunnyview Road
Libertyville, Ill.

Jaguar Owners Club
32 E. 57th St.
New York 22, N.Y.

Kissel Kar Klub
546 N. Main St.
Hartford, Wis.

Le Cerele Concourse
d'Elegance Bud Cohn
1323 Venice Blvd.
Los Angeles 6, Calif.

Lincoln-Continental Club
Elliston H. Bell, Jr.
245 State St.
Boston 9, Mass.

Lincoln Owners Club
735 Clinton Ave.
Bridgeport, Conn.

Locomobile Steamer Club
3321 Eastbrook Dr.
Fort Wayne, Ind.

Marmon Register
629 Orangewood Dr.
Dunedin, Fla.

Marmon V-16 Club
106 Tyler Terrace
Newton Center 59, Mass.

Mercedes-Benz Club of America
P.O. Box 4550
Chicago 80, Ill.

Mercer Associates
P.O. Box 25503
Los Angeles, Calif. 90025

MG Car Club Inc.
420 Madison Ave.
New York 17, N.Y.
(Richard S. Gilbert)

Model A Ford Restorers Club
William E. Hall
71 Lexington Road
West Hartford 7, Conn.

Model A Restorers Club
P.O. Box 1939
Dearborn, Mich.

Model T Ford Club
701 N. Michigan Ave.
Chicago 11, Ill.

Model T Ford Club
732 Ridge Ave.
Evanston, Ill.

National Assn. for Stock
Car Racing NASCAR
1801 Volusia Ave.
Daytona Beach, Fla.

National Hot Rod Association
3418 W. 1st St.
Los Angeles, Calif. 90004

Packard Auto Classics
P.O. Box 2808
Oakland 18, Calif.

Packard Motor Car Club
P.O. Box 618
Berkeley 1, Calif.

Pierce-Arrow Society
146 Vassar St.
Rochester, N.Y. 14607

Pierce-Arrow Society
Peter V. R. Lapey
69 Berkley Place
Buffalo 2, N.Y.

Pioneer Automobile Assn.
2222 Sample St.
South Bend, Ind.

Plymouth Owners Club
Jay M. Fisher
Hilltop Circle
Brookside, N.J.

Renault Owners Club
P.O. Box 1070
Hollywood, Calif.

Rickenbacker Club
P.O. Box 448
Bryan, Ohio

Rolls-Royce Club
D. D. Williams
622 Woodburn Road
Raleigh, N.C.

Singer Owners' Club
R. J. Van Laanen
11577 Laurel Crest Dr.
Studio City, Calif.

The Small Auto Club
1717 Walnut St.
Philadelphia 3, Pa.

Southern California Timing Assoc.
Bonneville Speed Trials
9607 Poinciana St.
Pico Rivera, Calif. 90660

Sports Car Club of America
P.O. Box 791
Westport, Conn.

Steam Car Owners Club
Box 335 R
Staten Island 8, N.Y.

Studebaker Drivers Club
30 Chicago Ave.
Bellmore, N.Y. 11712

Thunderbird Club of America
Jack McLean
P.O. Box 345
Dearborn, Mich.

Tucker Torpedo Club
4000 King Richard Dr.
Corpus Christi, Tex.

United States Auto Club
P.O. Box 1555
Indianapolis 6, Ind.

U.S. Kart Assn. Inc.
615 N. Delaware St.
Indianapolis 2, Ind.

Veteran Motor Car Club
15 Newton St.
Brookline 46, Mass.

Vintage Chevrolet Club
15933 Arminta St.
Van Nuys, Calif.

Waltham-Orient Club
617 West Broward
Fort Lauderdale, Fla.

Wills Ste. Claire Club
705 South Clyde Ave.
Kissimmee, Fla.

Willys-Knight Club
1407 Stirling Ave.
Dallas 16, Tex.

Index